find it
keep it

**The Guardian/NUS Guide
to Student Finance**

CW01551811

find it
keep it

The Guardian / NUS Guide to Student Finance

Jimmy Leach

national union of students

Atlantic Books
London

First published in 2004 by Atlantic Books,
on behalf of Guardian Newspapers Ltd.
Atlantic Books is an imprint of Grove Atlantic Ltd.

The Guardian is a registered trademark of the Guardian Media Group Plc.

Guardian Books is an imprint of Guardian Newspapers Ltd.

10 9 8 7 6 5 4 3 2 1

A CIP catalogue record for this book
is available from the British Library

ISBN 1 84354 318 4

Printed in Great Britain

Grove Atlantic Ltd
Ormond House
26–27 Boswell Street
London WC1N 3JZ

Contents

Part 1 **Find it**

Money to help you study, and how to find it

7

Initial Teacher Training

Graduate Teacher Programme
    (GTP) 75

BEd 72
Basic support 72
Discretionary support 72

**Registered Teacher
    Programme** 75

PGCE 73

**Repayment of Teacher's Loans
    (RTL)** 75

Added incentives 73
Teacher training salary 73
Fast Track programme 74
'Golden hello' 74

8

Part-time students

Tuition fees 77

Means test 77
Part-time student course grant 78
Disabled Students' Allowances
    for part-time students 78
Access to Learning Funds 78

Changing courses 79
Transferring courses 79
Converting from full- to part-time
    study 79
Conversion from part- to full-time
    study 79

Part-time students in Scotland 80
Tuition fees 80
Part-time student loan 80
Means test 80

**Part-time students in
    Northern Ireland** 81

Postgraduate support 81

Part-time study and benefits 81

Income Support 82

Jobseeker's Allowance (JSA) 82

9

Alternative financial assistance 83

10

Access to Learning Funds 87

11

European Union students 95

12

International students

13

Postgraduates

14

Further education students

Part 2 **Keep it**

Holding on to your cash and spending it wisely

1

Money 135

2

Earn while you learn 147

3

Tax 151

4

Health 165

5

Housing 179

6

Council Tax 193

7

Dealing with debt 199

Don't bury your head in the sand 199

Relearn budgeting 199
Talk 199
Prioritise 200
Change 200
Don't panic! 200
Credit agencies 201

Bankruptcy 204

Appendix 1

Local Education Authorities and their equivalents 205

England and Wales 205
Scotland 221
Northern Ireland 221

Appendix 2

Useful contacts 223

Acknowledgements 233

Index 234

For the purposes of this book, university isn't about studying. While we're together in these pages, we don't care, frankly, if you sleep in till lunchtime, miss all of your lectures, and only heave yourself out of your grubby pit of a bed in time to crack open the ginger nuts and watch *Columbo*. We don't mind if you fail to read the entire works of Charles Dickens in time for your tutorial and find yourself having to kick a copy of *Hard Times* about your room in an effort to make it look well-thumbed. If you want to indulge in classic student slacker behaviour, that's fine by us; you won't find us peering over our glasses disapprovingly.

While we're between these covers, all we care about is money. The only facts we want you to inwardly digest are those about the cash that could come your way: that the new tuition fees regime doesn't start till 2006; that there are three main tiers to the current system of financial support (a grant for fees, a grant for higher education students and the student loans); and that there's a whole host of other possibilities.

Many of you will be living away from home for the first time in your life and revelling in the alcopop-drinking, takeaway-munching, daft-clothes-buying opportunities that this brings. A university or college is a fantastic chance to meet friends you'll have for life, find new interests and obsessions and investigate all that the world has to offer. It is – to be blunt and a tad pretentious – a chance to be who you want to be. We're not going to tell you that university will definitely be the best days of your life, but it certainly has that potential.

But the biggest drag on this new life will be money. To see the places and people you want to, to buy the books you need to read and to live somewhere warm and dry costs money. And often, quite a lot of it. Most of you will not have wealthy parents whom you can sponge off for the next few years, so you'll need all the help you can get. You've probably heard a lot of debt scare stories, and estimates as to what you'll owe by the time you qualify vary from £10,000 to £30,000 (the latter for medical students, admittedly), but whatever happens, the chances are you'll be paying for your education long into your working life.

So this is your best chance to minimise the financial grief you'll endure for the foreseeable future. You can work out whether you are eligible – and how to claim – for the variety of funding options available to you (see **Find It**, from page 7), as well as the best ways to keep hold of that money (**Keep It**, from page 133). We're not encouraging you to be an avaricious gatherer of every last penny and to hoard your cash in a miserly fashion, but there are opportunities out there for you to get what you need and deserve, and we're trying to top that off with just a smidgeon of common sense.

Sadly, not all the answers are in this book. Everyone's personal circumstances differ, so what your mate down the corridor is claiming may not be applicable to you. Often we can only point you in the direction of your local education authority (LEA) or the student loans company (SLC), and then it's form-filling à gogo for you. But we can help you confirm that, yes, you are able to claim that money, or give you ammunition for an appeal against some bureaucratic cock-up that has left you eating tins of budget spaghetti again. But, armed with this, make sure you claim every penny – you'll be paying tax for the whole of your working life (and the student loan for a chunk of it), so don't feel guilty about taking from the State.

And once you've got it, be careful with it; don't go for every gaudy offer leaflet that the banks, credit card and mobile phone companies throw at you. Be sensible with your commitments and keep an eye on your spending, and you won't spend the next few years fretting about your finances.

The basics are quite simple. The details, however, can be pretty complicated, so concentrate now...

It might be hard to understand why the National Union of Students (NUS) is an advocate for the benefits of education when the negative implications of the cost of being a student at college or university and the consequential hardship and debt have been hitting the headlines all year.

However, the NUS firmly believes that education, at whatever level, can be and is frequently the key to a better life for millions of people across the United Kingdom. Research shows that education and training are significantly linked to the level of unemployment, where low literacy and low mathematical ability are associated with long-term unemployment. Similarly, poor or low-level qualifications are associated with an increased risk of long-term unemployment.

As a national movement whose very existence is determined by our members' place in the education system, we recognise the benefits and opportunities that education offers. We know that education, whether further or higher, post-16 or postgraduate, is a vital element in building a society free from poverty, ill health and discrimination. Without a strong and accessible education system, the structures of our society would collapse – no teachers, no doctors, no services and no future.

It is in everyone's best interests to ensure that our education sectors are accessible to all and that anyone, regardless of their financial or social background, can further their education, learning and skills.

But education is not just about degrees or qualifications. Being a student offers the opportunity to develop life skills, to meet new people from a wide range of different backgrounds and life experiences, to participate in new activities and to play an active role in the academic and local community.

The NUS campaign against top-up fees has demonstrated how students can participate in the democratic structures of our society. All year, students have lobbied their MPs in surgeries and at Parliament, have organised and turned out on demonstrations in London and across the country, met with their local councils to pass policy against variable fees at a local level, responded to government consultations and been shining examples of active and political citizens. Never has the citizenship agenda been pushed so strongly than this turbulent year, and from the war in Iraq to the anti-fascist campaign in local and European elections and the possibility of a general election in 2005, we fully expect students to maintain their role as political activists.

Institutions need to recognise that education is not just about lectures and academic work, and they need to make provision for student activities and development outside the classroom. Whether students want to be part of a sports team, get involved in student union activities or volunteer in the community, they need the active support and encouragement of the institution. Only by looking beyond the traditional boundaries of academia will our education sectors develop a positive understanding of the student experience and how new skills can have a positive impact on their students' employability.

Education is about the whole experience and we need to ensure that we, as politicians and leaders, as students and as the student movement, are working towards a positive change for social advance.

Over the past few years we have witnessed a dramatic change in the student demographic, with more adults and student parents returning to education, particularly in the further education system, as well as a shift towards vocational courses and 'sandwich' degrees. Any change that has a positive impact on the participation of non-traditional students can only be good for colleges and universities, good for the student experience and good for society.

However, as the NUS will continue to emphasise, any change needs proper support and funding so that non-traditional learners are not abandoned on the wayside.

Nevertheless, we must never take the 'bums-on-seats' attitude, which would be extremely damaging for students and their institutions. Quality of experience is the key, and from a student perspective we need to balance widening participation with dedicated, formal support for students as learners and as members of their communities.

Although we would like to see colleges and universities – and the government – take more responsibility for the welfare of their students, we also recognise that student support and development is not just an issue for institutions. The NUS and our student unions have a huge role to play in this area, and while unions should have the full backing of their parent institution, they should also be given the room to offer the support and assistance that students all too frequently require.

Students are often under great pressure, be it academic, financial or personal, and the ability to discuss issues and seek assistance from their peers is a wonderful, positive and extremely effective service on offer from the overwhelming majority of student unions.

The NUS is proud of its active and historical role in empowering student unions to offer the services and support that students so desperately need. Our mission statement is a bold vision constantly to improve the lives and experiences of students in the United Kingdom by ensuring their voice is heard and effectively represented by developing democratic and strong students' unions, and by providing collective benefits and access to information for all students.

We work on a grass-roots level through our student unions to ensure not only that the student experience is as broad as possible, but that students can access the information and support they need to continue their education.

We encourage student unions to have directly elected welfare officers and we offer research, representation, training and expert advice so that they can provide a service that really delivers for students.

We work with unions to run our national campaigns on a local level, to educate students on a wide range of concerns, from education funding, their rights as citizens, health and welfare matters, the environment, human rights, HIV/AIDS, student housing, women's rights, anti-racism, lesbian, gay and bisexual equality, disability equality and international issues.

Throughout the summer months we train student officers on a wide range of courses to meet the needs of sabbaticals in their varied roles, so that they are fully prepared to meet the needs of their students once they return from the summer break. Not only do these courses give the officers the information they require, they also provide a wonderful opportunity for networking and exchanging ideas. After all, if a campaign has worked in one student union, there is no reason why it can't be adapted to suit the needs of another. At a time of financial crisis for students, student unions and academic institutions, the reinvention of the wheel has never seemed so ludicrous.

As a campaigning organisation we make campaigns our priority, by using our collective voice and strengths to achieve real change. It's not all about lobbying the government; campaigns are necessary at a local level too, and the NUS prides itself on the work it has done with students and activists. Sometimes, success is easy to measure, but more often than not the student movement fails to take note of its achievements. When we campaign to ensure that further education student unions receive a decent amount of funding from their college so that they can run campaigns – or even work out of an office with proper equipment; when we set up new positions on union executive committees to represent black students, lesbian, gay or bisexual students, students with disabilities or women students; when we lobby institutions to keep Wednesday afternoons free for student activities; when we fight against department closures or hidden course costs; when we provide training for course reps; when we achieve improvements in lighting on campus; when we win on issues that seem small to us, but have a massive impact on the day-to-day lives of students, then we have won, and we have won together.

The NUS is a collective organisation with a collective voice fighting for collective benefits. That is why we are a national union – because only together can we win. Unity truly is our strength, and in these days of privatisation, with our education system up for sale to the highest bidder, it is our unity that we are relying on. Together, there are more of us than there are of them – and they wouldn't be where they are without the kind of education system that we are fighting for.

Education is a right, not a privilege, and of all the wonderful opportunities that we are offered throughout our lives, this is surely one of the greatest. To quote Nelson Mandela: 'Education is the most powerful weapon which you can use to change the world.'

Kat Fletcher, President of the National Union of Students, 2004/5

Part 1
Find it

Money to help you study,
and how to find it

1 Financial support for undergraduates

It's all change from 2006, when the tuition fees kick in (please don't tell us you were one of those who thought they'd already started...). The current system for full-time undergraduates in England and Wales dates from 1998 and applies to all those who began their course as 'new' students on or after 1 September 1998. For those of you who don't trust us and want to do the research yourselves, the relevant parliamentary regulations for 2004/5 are the Education (Student Support) (No.2) Regulations 2002 as amended by the Amendment Regulations 2004. Go on then, have a look...

If you began your studies before 1 September 1998 we are, frankly, going to ignore you. You've managed perfectly well without us so far, so the chances are you can get by for a bit longer. But if you've suddenly become a bit befuddled by your student finances or if you've been living on grass for eight years or so and have only just realised there's a better way, then contact your local NUS representative.

And for those in Scotland and Northern Ireland, hang on, we're getting to you in a bit (or go straight to page 49 for Scotland and page 57 for Northern Ireland, if you're the impatient sort).

■ The bottom line

Here we go (for those of you who are just flicking through this in a bookshop): a round-up of what an undergraduate is entitled to for the financial year 2004/5.

Tuition fee support

The maximum fee charged is currently £1,150. This is means-tested on your income and, if appropriate, the income of your parents or your husband/wife/cohabiting partner. If that combined income is below the applicable threshold, no fees are charged to you (see pages 29–30). Grants for fees are non-repayable. Think of it as a gift, not a loan. More details on pages 19–20.

Student loan

You are also eligible for a loan from the Student Loans Company at the following rates (more on pages 41–2):

- Living away from home, studying in London
  Full year: £5,050
  Final year: £4,380
- Living away from home, studying outside London
  Full year: £4,095
  Final year: £3,555
- Living at home
  Full year: £3,240
  Final year: £2,830

Twenty-five per cent of the student loan is means-tested, so you may not get it all, but everything that you borrow, you pay back.

If you have to attend your courses for longer than 30 weeks and three days, you are entitled to an additional loan to cover living costs at a weekly rate of:

- Living away from home, studying in London: £94
- Living away from home, studying outside London: £73
- Living at home: £49

Higher Education Grant

If you are a new student and your family is on a low income, a grant of up to £1,000 is available. This is means-tested on your family's household income and is non-repayable.

Supplementary grants

Other non-repayable grants include:

- childcare grants
- Parents' Learning Allowance

- Disabled Students' Allowance (DSA)

- grants for travel

- and a grant for students who have been in custody or care prior to entering higher education and who are under 21 on the first day of the course.

■ New elements to your student support

For those of you who have been paying attention to undergraduate financial support systems (or more likely have a brother or sister studying already), you'll find that from September 2004 there will be a few changes to full-time undergraduate student support. In short, these are:

- **A new higher education (HE) grant of up to £1,000** has been introduced to help those from low-income backgrounds. There has already been something similar for Welsh students (the Assembly Learning Grant), but from now on, the grant will cover all students in England and Wales. Students in Scotland and Northern Ireland, do not sigh in exasperation – we'll get to you later in the book.

- Those expecting a contribution from their parents (or a husband or wife) will be pleased to know that there will be a **higher income threshold for parental/spouse contribution scales** – your parents or spouse now have to be earning more than before if they are expected to give you some money. This is good news, since fewer of you will be expected to go cap-in-hand to your parents/husband/wife, but bear in mind that the income of your mum/dad/partner (married or just living together) will be added to the equation too and be part of the means test.

- There is a **system of 'disregards'** for the means tests (i.e., the bits they don't care about), which **has been substantially altered and simplified**. For example, single independent students will now be able to earn up to £10,000 before it is taken into account in means tests.

- The **hardship funds** you may have heard about **will be replaced by Access to Learning Funds**. The Hardship Loan will be abolished, as will Opportunity Bursaries.

In general, the rates of financial support you receive and the income thresholds for the means tests will increase in line with inflation – the figure for which is taken from the Retail Price Index (which the Department for Education and Skills estimates at 2.4 per cent for 2004). But you should note that two elements of student support (the details of which you'll find on page 68) have not been upgraded for 2004/5:

- **Payments from the Childcare Grant**
- **The Care Leaver's Grant.**

■ Are you eligible?

To qualify for grants, loans and tuition-fee support, you have to be a bona fide student doing a bona fide course, so both you and you course need to meet certain criteria.

Personal eligibility

To qualify for cash, you must fall into one of these categories:

- **You must be settled in the UK on the first day of the first academic year** of the course and must have been 'ordinarily resident' in the UK (that is, you haven't come here just to study) for the three years running up to the first day of the first year of your course.

There are exemptions to this rule. If, for example, you have been absent from the UK during any part of those required three years because of your parents' or your own temporary employment abroad (including the armed forces) or occasional absences for holidays or if you or your family is from the European Union (or Switzerland) or if you are an officially recognised refugee.

- **You must have 'settled' status in the UK** – i.e., there must be no restrictions stamped in your passport regarding the length of your stay in the UK. Again, there are exemptions – for refugees and asylum seekers (and their families) and EU (or Swiss) students.

- There is no age restriction for fee support, but **you must be aged under 50 at the beginning of your course** to be eligible for the student loan, the grant, and other supplementary grants (with the exception of the Disabled Students' Allowance). If you are over 50 but under 55 at the beginning of your course, you are eligible for student loans and grants only if you make a firm commitment to enter or return to employment on completing your course.

You may feel you are eligible, but it's not just about you – your course must qualify too. Now, the chances are that you don't have to fret. Most 'ordinary' courses at 'ordinary' institutions qualify, so if you got your university place through UCAS or the clearing process you probably have nothing to worry about. If you have any doubts, check with the admissions tutor.

The criteria are:

- **You must be attending a 'designated' course** – i.e., a first degree course, courses of Higher National Diploma (HND); a Diploma of Higher Education (DipHE) or Higher National Certificate (HNC); employment-related two-year foundation degree courses; medical, dental and veterinary science courses (including intercalated first degree – a BSc for example); full-time or part-time courses of Initial Teacher Training (ITT) including PGCE and courses for further training of teachers or youth and community workers.

■ Could you be the odd one out?

If you clear the eligibility hurdles, you will be able to claim for financial support for fees, maintenance loans and supplementary grants, and then jump the next set of hurdles of the income assessment test (or means test). However, you may feel there is something about your personal circumstances that might affect your chances of getting the money. Hopefully, we can deal with a few of those right now...

If you have previously enrolled on a course, this might affect your entitlement for financial help with your fees and your grant (and not for the better), but it will not affect your entitlement to the student loan and supplementary grants.

You will be excluded from financial assistance if you come under one of the following categories:

- **If you have previously attended a full-time course** of higher education for longer than one academic year at a publicly funded institution (this can apply to private institutions as well, if they received assistance from public funds).

- **If you received support from public funds** to meet the costs of fees during your previous attempt at study.

Now, you may get away with it (and still get the financial support) if your previous attempt at study lasted just one academic year (and not a day over) or if your second course is a full-time course of Initial Teacher Training (ITT), which doesn't last longer than two years (or its part-time equivalent) and leads to your becoming a qualified teacher.

You should also be OK if you had a compelling reason not to finish your course last time – i.e., if you were too ill to continue or you had to care for someone in your family.

From sub- to full degrees

You should start getting used to sub-clauses and exemptions, because there are plenty of them – and here's another. If you have attended a 'sub-degree' HE course, such as a HND or a DipHE, and now wish to embark on a three- or four-year degree course, you are eligible for a reduced entitlement for a grant for fees for the final year or years of your new course.

So if you end up studying for longer than normal, you don't get to take the money with you for the extra – and that's the case even if you did an accelerated two-year first degree course. If you're not sure how long the support will last and you need to know before you start the course, then contact your local NUS office and they can investigate on your behalf.

PGCE students

If you are doing a Postgraduate Certificate of Education (PGCE) you are exempt from paying fees, but are still entitled to a full year's loan. Which is nice.

If you're doing a flexible PGCE course, you will have your tuition fees paid by the Teacher Training Agency (TTA), assuming the TTA recognises and approves the course. If you are on a flexible PGCE course that has *not* been approved by the TTA, you will not have your fees paid and will have to apply for fee support in the usual way. If the flexible PGCE course is less than one academic year in duration you are not eligible for any living costs support.

There are additional incentives for Initial Teacher Training at postgraduate level – see pages 73–4 for details.

For further details, contact the Teaching Information Line on 0845 6000 991 or 0845 6000 992 (the Welsh language line) or visit **www. useyourheadteach.gov.uk**.

Transferring courses

The Government takes particular care over your right to financial support in the event of your asking to change your course, not necessarily on educational grounds (and let's assume it's done with the full consent of the receiving academic authority).

You can still get the money, but your new institution must notify your Local Education Authority (LEA) of the transfer (and it'll do no harm to politely remind them of that).

The basic rules for course transfers are:

- **If you transfer within one academic year** from the beginning of your original course, you remain entitled to the normal financial package of support with fees, supplementary grants and the student loan during the entire duration of the new course.

- **If you transfer after being on a course for longer than one academic year**, you are eligible for support for the whole duration of whichever is the longer course (either the first or the second one). However, if your combined period of attendance on both courses exceeds the duration of whichever course is the longer, you will not be eligible for support for the duration of the excess academic year(s).

To save you re-reading that sentence, try this: **if you change in the second year of a three-year course to another three-year course, your entitlements remain at three years' worth**. If you are on a sandwich course, periods of work experience are disregarded when calculating the length of the courses. So if you're out working somewhere for a year, that's irrelevant (thankfully) for the purposes of this calculation. The unsupported years are always the earliest year or years of the second course. Your entitlement to a student loan is not affected by transfer between courses.

You should also note that, although Universities UK (the group combining all university vice-chancellors) recommends that institutions charge pro-rata fees for students who transfer during an academic year, theoretically both universities could charge you the maximum fee for the whole academic year, even if you spend one term at one and two at another. Worth checking before you jump ship...

Repeat years

If you repeat your first year or part of it, you remain eligible for fee support and for the grant, although repeat repeating isn't necessarily a good idea: fee and grant support for a subsequent repeat of either the first year or part of it, or of any other year of your course, is at the LEA's discretion.

Despite the fact that a repeat year effectively extends the length of your course, you remain entitled to continued financial support for living costs and for the grant for fees during the extended period required to complete the course.

If you repeat a year or part of a year of your course on a part-time basis, you will retain the same eligibility for financial support that you were granted when you initially enrolled on a full-time course. However, if you transfer officially on to a part-time course you will no longer be eligible for full-time support for any following years of study.

Suspending your studies

It may be that you have to suspend your studies for personal or family reasons – so you may need to leave your course, but intend to return at a later date. You should notify your LEA without delay and, if possible, you should let the LEA know an approximate date for your return to the course, but bear in mind that suspension stretching to years is unlikely to be accepted. The LEA will then suspend your eligibility for financial support – grant for fees, grant, loan and supplementary grants – until the time you start to attend the course again.

Students who suspend their studies but who return to the course during the same term are still charged fees for the whole term. Loans and supplementary grants are not generally paid to you during your time away from the course unless you are ill. However, the LEA may take into account your reasons for suspension and exercise their discretion in favour of paying either a portion – or the whole amount – of loan, grant and supplementary allowances. It's up to them, so be nice.

Ill health

If you're unlucky enough to be ill, but lucky enough to be ill for fewer than 60 days, that period of absence does not affect your entitlement to the student loan. If an absence due to illness extends beyond 60 days, the institution you are attending usually notifies the Student Loans Company, which then stops further loan instalments being paid to you. However, if you do not abandon your course but are likely to face extreme hardship (depending on the reasons for your absence), your college or university, in agreement with the LEA, may take into account the additional financial hardship which the non-payment of the loan instalment would cause and authorise further payments to you. A letter of support from your education institution may help to satisfy the LEA that you intend to return to the course.

Withdrawing from your course

If you leave or abandon your course, you should notify your LEA without delay. Your eligibility for loan, supplementary grants and grant for fees depends on you actually undertaking a course, so when you stop you're no longer entitled, obviously. Once you tell the LEA that you've given up on your education, they will instruct the Student Loans Company to stop payments of loan, grant, supplementary grants and tuition fees, as students are not entitled to apply for further financial support after they withdraw from a course. Don't try to be clever and keep the money coming in. They'll just claim it back and you'll look a chump.

■ Fees, loans and grants

So, you've been through the previous section, and yes, you're eligible – but now you know that, what can you apply for? Just how much is coming your way? And how do you get it?

■ The application process

You apply for almost all your financial support (fees grant, the HE grant, the student loan and all other Government grants) through your local education authority (LEA). You'll use the same system for all the money you'll be trying to squeeze out of them.

Very briefly, there is now only one form for you to complete either on paper or online (although there are separate forms for new and continuing courses). The LEA enters the data into the system, makes its decisions and then informs you, via the Student Loans Company of what they are, and payments are arranged from there. This includes Disabled Students' Allowance, although in this case the LEA usually sends out a separate form if you notify them of a disability on the first form. On that first form you also indicate whether or not you would like a student loan. You can see what the form looks like here: **www.dfes. gov.uk/studentsupport/formsandguides/for_forms.shtml**.

From the January prior to the start of a course you can approach your local LEA to get an application form. Forms can also be downloaded from the DfES's website at **www.dfes.gov.uk/studentsupport**.

Alternatively, you can apply online at **www.studentfinancedirect.co.uk** and the form will be sent to your LEA for you. Based on the information submitted on the form, the LEA will assess your personal eligibility for financial support, and then what funding you are entitled to.

Although most students will have the first instalment of the loan paid straight into their bank or building society account, in some institutions you may be required to collect a cheque from your institution. All further instalments will, however, be electronically transferred.

All requested information should be returned to the LEA by their specified deadlines to ensure that you receive the first instalment of loan and any supplementary grants you are entitled to at the start of your course.

But you should **start the process as soon as you can** – don't wait for your final exam results to come through (even if it means you don't know which university you'll be going to yet). The process can take weeks, months even, so if you wait till August, you'll most likely be scuppered when it comes to buying that first round on your first night out with your new friends. So **if you intend to start your course in September, send in the form by the end of the preceding June** at the very latest if you're a new student, and by the end of May if you are continuing.

The loan will usually be paid in three instalments, assuming you get your application in nice and early. It will be paid by BACS transfer, so make sure you've got a bank account open and ready.

- [✓] Apply to your Local Education Authority from January
- [✓] Complete the application form to see if you're eligible for help towards your tuition fees and/or a student loan
- [✓] Apply to the Student Loans Company as early as you can
- [✓] Get the bank account ready

■ Grants for tuition fees

Assuming you pass all of the above tests and you and your course are eligible, you will be entitled to a maximum of £1,150 in the means-tested grant for tuition fees. This grant includes admission, registration, tuition and graduation fees and is paid on your behalf by the Student Loans Company.

For **sandwich courses** (fewer than ten weeks of full-time study) and **part-time courses** of Initial Teacher Training, the maximum tuition fees payable are £560.

For courses at institutions not maintained or assisted from public funds, the maximum tuition fees payable are £1,075. There are, of course, exceptions, which are:

- Buckingham University: £2,705
- The Guildhall School of Music: £4,150
- Heythrop College: £2,045.

Most fees are means-tested on your income and that of your parents or husband/wife/partner, so you may not get the maximum (for full details, see the section on means-testing on page 29). If the means test decides that you should make no contribution and your LEA should pay the entire amount, the student loans people will pay the fees on your behalf, up to the applicable maximum level, directly to the institution.

■ Self-financing students

Colleges and universities can charge higher fees to self-financing students. They are often students outside the European Union (EU), but can also be those students who are not eligible for a grant for fees owing to previous attendance or who do not qualify under the 'eligibility' rules (see page 12) or who have simply not applied for financial assessment.

The last is likely to be the most relevant to you – make sure you are assessed for eligibility for financial support by your LEA, even if you think you're too posh and your family income excludes you from the grant or a grant for fees. That way, you make sure you don't qualify as an 'award'-holding student and thereby risk being charged fees above £1,150.

■ Student loans

Twenty-five per cent of your loan is means-tested and loans are paid in three instalments if applied for within the first quarter of the year (so make sure you do – it makes life a lot less complicated).

Here is a list of the maximum amounts of loan that eligible students are entitled to claim for the year 2004/5:

Full year

- Living away from home, studying in London
  £5,050 – of which £1,260 is means-tested
- Living away from home, studying outside London
  £4,095 – of which £1,025 is means-tested
- Living at the parental home (London or elsewhere)
  £3,240 – of which £810 is means-tested

Final year

- Living away from home, studying in London
  £4,380 – of which £1,095 is means-tested
- Living away from home, studying outside London
  £3,555 – of which £890 is means-tested
- Living at parental home (London or elsewhere)
  £2,830 – of which £705 is means-tested

■ Overseas study 2004/5

If you're really sophisticated and attend an overseas institution (for at least eight weeks) as a necessary part of your course, you are entitled to a higher rate of loan:

Full year
£5,000 – of which £1,250 is means-tested
Final year
£4,350 – of which £1,085 is means-tested

■ Non-means-tested (reduced rate) loans

If you are on the following courses, you are eligible for non-means-tested, reduced-rate loans:

- **Part-time Initial Teacher Training courses** with less than six weeks' full-time attendance (see the section on teacher training on page 71)
- **Full-year paid or unpaid placements** of sandwich courses
- **NHS bursary holders** (see the section on healthcare students on page 61)

The rates for you if you're included in the above are:

- Living away from home, studying in London
  Full year: £2,480
  Final year: £1,810

- Living away from home, studying outside London
  Full year: £2,005
  Final year: £1,465

- Living at the parental home
  Full year: £1,535
  Final year: £1,125

■ Hardship loans

Hardship loans for all students will be abolished from September 2004. If you are in financial difficulty you should approach your institution's Access to Learning Fund for additional assistance. (See Access to Learning Funds on page 87).

■ The Higher Education Grant

If you start a new course in September 2004 or later, you will be eligible for the shiny new Higher Education Grant of up to £1,000. It is means-tested and the maximum amount of £1,000 will be available to you if your household income is assessed to be £15,200 or lower. If you have a household income of less than £21,185 you will receive a partial grant on a sliding scale; the grant is reduced by £1 for every £6.30 by which the household income is greater than £15,200.

It seems a weird calculation, but there you go. It means that if you have a household income of, for example, £18,000, you would receive a grant of £636. See the section on the means test starting on page 29 and then find your calculator if you want to work it out for yourself.

Students on full-time, sandwich, and part-time initial teacher-training courses will be eligible to apply for this new grant. Sadly, if you started your course before September 2004 you won't be eligible.

■ Grants for parents

Childcare Grant

The Childcare Grant **is based on the actual cost of the childcare incurred** by a student parent. To be eligible you must first, of course, have a child, but you must also use registered or approved childcare for the little perisher. This grant cannot be used to pay for informal arrangements (you can't expect them to pay granny for looking after junior).

The LEA will pay up to 85 per cent of a student's weekly childcare costs, with a maximum payment of £114.75 a week for one child and a maximum payment of £170 a week for two or more children. These costs can be claimed for the entire academic year (including the long vacation), not just during term-time. Students in their final year can claim up until the last day of their final term.

The **financial assessment form** from the LEA will ask if you would like any help with childcare costs. Tick yes and you will receive some further info and an application form for the childcare grant. Fill this in and ask your carer to complete the **confirmation form** with their details and confirmation of the amounts they receive from you. Keep receipts for the amount you pay the carer, because the LEA will want them (usually in February) to verify you are being paid correctly. Any over or under-payments will be adjusted in future instalments of the grant, which you will receive in three instalments alongside your student loan payments. If the figures are badly out and the overpayment is more than you are due to receive (i.e., you owe them), then that money could be taken from your Parents' Learning Allowance (see below). Your LEA will let you know.

If you are unable to pay any remaining childcare costs, you should approach your university's or college's Access to Learning Fund for further support

And one more piece of good news: the Childcare Grant is not taken into account as income in the calculation of means-tested social security benefits.

Parents' Learning Allowance (PLA)

The Parents' Learning Allowance is intended to help cover course-related costs **for students with dependent children**. How much you get depends on your household income and, again, it is not counted as income when assessing means-tested social security benefit entitlement.

The maximum entitlement in 2003/4 is £1,330.

You can claim the PLA if you are in full-time education and either:

- you are, in principle, eligible for the Childcare Grant and/or the Adult Dependants' Grant (see below), even if you do not actually receive any funds from either because your dependants' income is too high

or

- you have dependent children, but no adult dependants and are not eligible for the Childcare Grant because you are not using approved or registered childcare.

If you are eligible, the amount you receive will vary according to your dependants' income. Students will receive the full £1,330 if their dependants' income is less than:

- £3,070 for a couple with one child
- £4,095 for a couple with two or more children
- £4,095 for a lone parent with one child
- £5,120 for a lone parent with two or more children

Where any dependants' income is higher than this the PLA is reduced, pound for pound, to a minimum of £50. If your dependants' income is more than £1,330 over the above thresholds, you will receive nothing.

If you are part of a couple and you are both full-time students, you can both claim the full PLA, subject to the income thresholds

You apply for the allowance as part of your normal income assessment form when you will be asked for details of any dependants you have. The money will be paid in three instalments in the same manner as, and alongside, your student loan payment.

■ Further grants and awards

Adult Dependants' Grant

If you have adult dependants 'wholly or mainly financially dependent' on you (your husband/wife may be unable to earn, for example), you may be able to claim the Adult Dependants' Grant.

The maximum grant available in 2004/5 is £2,335, but the amount you receive depends on your income and that of your dependants. You can have income up to the following levels without it being taken into account in the means test:

- £1,025 if you have no dependent children
- £3,070 if you have a spouse or partner and one dependent child
- £4,095 if you have a spouse or partner and more than one dependent child
- £4,095 if you are a lone parent and have one dependent child
- £5,120 if you are a lone parent and have more than one dependent child.

As with the PLA, you apply for the Adult Dependants' Grant as part of your normal income assessment form, when you will be asked for details of any dependants you have. The money will be paid in three instalments in the same manner as, and alongside, your student loan payment.

Grants for travel costs

If you study medicine and dentistry and incur additional travel expenditure to attend a hospital or other premises as part of your clinical training, you are eligible for a grant to cover any travel costs beyond a total of £275 during the academic year.

Similarly, **if you attend an overseas institution** as a necessary part of your course for at least eight weeks, you are entitled to a grant for any travel costs that are in excess of £275.

In both cases the first £275 is to be paid by you. If you have difficulty in affording that bottom-line figure, you should approach your university's Access to Learning Fund for assistance.

Disabled Students' Allowance (DSA)

If you are disabled and end up incurring additional course-related costs as a consequence of your disability, you can apply for the following allowances (the rates given are the maximum that an LEA can approve):

- For a non-medical personal helper
  £11,550 per academic year
- For major items of specialist equipment
  £4,565 for the duration of the course
- Other expenditure
  Up to £1,525 per academic year
- Travel expenditure incurred by attending the course
  Full reimbursement

DSAs are not means-tested, so students aged 55 or over with disabilities can apply for these allowances even if they are not eligible for student loans.

The LEA will look at all cases where you incur extra disability-related cost while studying, but you will need to provide them with medical proof of your disability or disabilities, such as a letter from a doctor, educational psychologist or other specialist

If you are eligible for a DSA you will be given a **needs assessment** to determine the level and nature of the support to be provided by the LEA. A list of recognised assessors should be sent to you along with notification that the LEA has agreed that you should be supported through the DSA. It's unusual for an assessment to be carried out before this agreement.

The cost of the assessment will be covered by the LEA, but the DSA cannot cover any expenses associated with the diagnosis of a disability (an educational psychologist's report, for example). If you require such a diagnosis but lack the ability to pay, you should approach your university's or college's Access to Learning Fund for assistance.

Although the DSA may be applied for at any stage during the course, you should apply as early as possible as the needs assessment process and the provision of any subsequent assistance or equipment can take several weeks.

The SLC will make payments of the DSA either straight into your bank account or straight to the provider of the specialist equipment or services.

Grants for students who left local authority care

If you are under the age of 21 at the start of your course and, as a result of a court order, were in custody or care before going to college or university, you are entitled to a maximum of £100 a week towards your accommodation costs during the long vacation only. Ask your LEA for details if they haven't already approached you.

However, this grant is being phased out: if you were aged 16 or 17 on 1 October 2001 or later and placed in care, a new scheme which will offer help during the shorter vacations as well as the long vacation has been set up, and in this case you should speak to your social worker or personal adviser for information.

The Welsh Assembly Learning Grant

If you started your further or higher education in either the 2002/3 or the 2003/4 academic years and lived in Wales for the three years before that, and you are on a low income, you may be eligible for a means-tested Assembly Learning Grant of up to £1,500.

A grant of at least £500 will be available if you are on a full-time HE course and your family income is below £15,000. The full £1,500 will be offered if you have an income of less than £5,000. The grants are administered through Welsh LEAs, but you can attend any institution in the UK.

If you are a Welsh student on a low income and starting your higher education in September 2004 or later you should apply for the new HE grant instead, but if you are on a very low income (assessed to be below £5,116), you may be given extra help through an Assembly Learning Grant. If you think you qualify, you should contact your LEA.

 Also see…

www.learning.wales.gov.uk
www.dysgu.cymru.gov.uk (Welsh language site)

Bursaries for Foyer residents

If you have been living in accommodation provided by the Foyer Federation (if you have to ask, it won't be you) or you were otherwise homeless, you will be given priority help from the Access to Learning Funds. For Foyer residents in particular there are bursaries of £1,000 a year to help cover vacation time accommodation costs.

Foyer residents should contact Garmon Apgarth at the Foyer Federation on 020 7430 2212 or e-mail garmon@foyer.net for more information on eligibility and how to apply.

2 The means test

■ **The income assessment test**

The Government has made most elements of student financial support means-tested. They expect that, after reaching a certain level of income, you or your household (most often, your parents) should contribute to the costs of your education and maintenance, both your fees and your upkeep. And there's no hiding place – if you or any relevant members of your household choose not to be means-tested, then your student loan and grant for tuition fees will be limited to 75 per cent of the maximum, since three quarters of the loan is offered independently of the test, and 25 per cent is contingent on the outcome of the assessment.

The way it works is this: on the application form you will need to answer questions about your income and your parents' or partner's income. From this data they will make the income assessment (more popularly known as the means test). From that information, and from the paperwork you attach to it (P60s perhaps, or payslips), they will make judgements as to the money available to you, both from your own sources and that of your parents or partner (i.e., the household income), whether you or your household are in a position to make a contribution towards your tuition fees. They will write to you and let you know.

The details are below, but the most important thing is this: if your household income is less than £21,475 you will get the full grant for tuition fees. If it's between £21,475 and £31,972 you will get a partial grant for fees. If your household income is £31,973 or more, there will be no grant for tuition fees and your entitlement to any supplementary grants and ultimately student loan starts to be reduced as well.

The new Higher Education Grant is also a means-tested affair and the maximum amount of £1,000 will be available to you if your household income is assessed to be £15,200 or less. If you have a household income of less than £21,185 you will receive a partial grant on a sliding scale; the grant is reduced by £1 for every £6.30 by which the household income is greater than £15,200. So if you have a household income of, for example, £18,000, you would receive a grant of £636.

■ What's your income?

In the calculation of your household income, just what counts?
The means test can include several different factors:

- **Your own income.** This means test applies in every case.

- **Your parents' income.** This applies if you are not exempted from the parental means test (i.e., you do not have 'independent' status – see below for details).

- **Your spouse's income.** This applies if you are married, but not separated at the beginning of the academic year

- **Your cohabiting partner's income.** This applies if you started your course in September 2000 or later, are aged 25 or over on the first day of the academic year and live with a heterosexual partner in a stable relationship. There's no need to debate the whys and wherefores of the phrasing of this last bit right now. It's the official line, so take it up with someone else.

In a means test all relevant income is combined to form a 'household income' figure which is used to assess the household's contribution to your student support. From that, they decide on what sort of grant, support for fees and student loan you can claim.

The level of assessed contribution of the rest of your household (most usually, the amount your parents are expected to chip in) will initially reduce the grant (if you are eligible for one), then the grant for fees, then any grants for your dependants, then the means-tested amount of student loan (which can be cut by 25 per cent of the maximum rate), followed finally by the reduction of any grants for travel costs you may be entitled to.

Your own income

The money you will make in an academic year is counted in the household income equation. The income on which you are assessed is that which you estimate to make during the academic year for which you are applying. All taxable sources of income should be included on the form, but any source of income that is not regarded as taxable is wholly ignored.

There is a system of **disregarded income**, which is basically the money you can earn that they don't care about. The very good news (and the bit you just started worrying about) is that in addition, although taxable, earnings from part-time or casual work undertaken during the academic year are also ignored.

Examples of disregarded income:

- All earnings from part-time or casual employment during the academic year
- Most scholarships and sponsorships
- Tax credits
- Non-taxable benefits (for example, Child Benefit, Housing Benefit, disability benefits, most payments of Income Support)
- Maintenance payments made to you by any person under a formal agreement
- An amount equivalent to any maintenance payments made by you in respect of your children or former partner
- £1,000 for each person under the age of 18 who is financially dependent on you

But there are some things which may apply which you should include:

- Income from trust funds
- Interest on savings
- Dividends on shares or taxable income from other investments
- Taxable benefits (for example, Jobseeker's Allowance, statutory sick pay, statutory maternity pay)
- Rent from property you let

The parental contribution

For the purposes of the means test, your parents will be counted as your natural or adoptive parents and, if your parents have separated, can now include the cohabiting heterosexual partner of an assessable parent (i.e., if you live with your mum, they'll count her live-in boyfriend's income too). Foster parents and guardians are not regarded as assessable.

If a parent dies during the financial year in which their income would have been assessed, both parents' income is means-tested up to the date of death, and the surviving parent's income only after the death of the other parent. In the event that your parents' marriage or cohabitation terminates during the year of assessment, the joint income is applied only up to the point of termination, and the parent with whom you continue to live will be assessed thereafter.

The income on which your parents are assessed is the gross taxable income for the last full tax year preceding the academic year for which you are applying for funding. For a student whose course commences on 1 September 2004, the financial or tax year (the preceding financial year) for which contributions will be assessed is from 5 April 2003 to 6 April 2004. The current financial year is 6 April 2004 to 5 April 2005.

However, if your parents' income during the current financial year is likely to drop by at least 15 per cent compared to that of the preceding financial year and it is unlikely to rise significantly, the LEA may reassess parental contribution based on an average of your parents' residual income for the current and the preceding financial year.

There are some opportunities for your parents to make the most of the system of **disregarded income**:

- any amount paid by your parent or parents into a pension scheme which attracts tax relief
- £1,000 for each child wholly or mainly dependent on your parents (other than yourself)
- £1,000 if your parent is also a full-time student.

If you have a brother or sister who is also a student, then the total amount of contributions your parents should make shall not exceed the amount of contribution that would be made if only one child held an award.

Although LEAs have discretion on the apportionment of contributions, it is usually divided equally between those award-holders (the student siblings), unless the LEA considers that a different proportion may be more equitable.

There are a few extra points we should add here to make a rather complex situation clearer:

- There's no law saying that if the LEA decides your parents have the cash to help you out and so reduce the level of support they give, then your parents have to make up the shortfall. You might have tightwad parents and there's not much anyone can do about it. Unless there is permanent estrangement from your parents (rather than a series of slanging matches), LEAs are unable to increase the support offered in the event that your parents choose not to contribute. If you find yourself in this position, seek help from the Access to Learning Fund, but note that the ALF will not simply cough up the amount your parents were supposed to provide, although where you are genuinely not being supported by your parents and this is causing you hardship, you will be considered sympathetically.

- If your parents choose not to disclose the necessary information to enable the LEA to determine whether a contribution is payable, you will receive only the minimum support to which you are eligible. So you'd better hope they make up the difference.

- If you attend only part of your course, the parental contribution is reduced pro rata.

- Where your parents are estranged and the parent assessed for contribution dies, the surviving parent will not be assessed for contribution. In such an unfortunate situation, different rules kick in and you'd best contact your LEA for advice.

Spouse or partner's income

If you are married by the time of the first day of the academic year, your husband or wife will be assessed for the purposes of the household income calculation for that academic year, rather than your parents.

If you started your course in September 2000 or later and are aged 25 or over, any cohabiting partner of the opposite sex can also be assessed (i.e., you don't have to be married for it to count). But if you are aged 24 or less and are not otherwise classed as an independent student (see below) you will still be subject to the parental means test, but your cohabiting partner will not be assessed.

The **income of spouses and cohabiting partners are assessed on the same basis as parents** (see above).

Where a marriage or cohabitation takes place or terminates during the assessment period, the means test is applied only for the number of weeks for which the marriage or cohabitation continued.

Independent students

You won't suffer the pleasures of the parental means test (you'll just be judged by your own and/or spouse's income) if you are classified as 'independent', which is a financial judgement, not one on your free spirit, and is defined by the following:

- you have reached the age of 25 before the beginning of the academic year
- You marry before the beginning of the academic year
- You have been 'self-supporting' for any three years before the academic year.

Alternatively, you are independent if:

- You are irreconcilably estranged from your parents; or have been in custody or care
- Your parents cannot be found or it is not reasonably practicable for your parents to send parental contributions to the UK
- Your parents live outside the EU and it is either not reasonably practicable for your parents to send parental contributions or it would place them in jeopardy.
- You are an orphan
- You are a member of a religious order residing in a house of that order.

Self-supporting

Self-support is rather similar to 'independent' in that it means parental income won't be assessed. It means you have supported yourself out of your earnings for an aggregate of three years before starting your course. In addition, the following criteria are accepted as evidence of self-support:

- Any period of registered unemployment and availability for employment
- Any period when you were in receipt of benefit payable in respect of a person who is unemployed (by which they mean Income Support or Jobseeker's Allowance)
- Any period when you were participating in any scheme of training for the unemployed
- Any period when you were in receipt of any benefit or allowance or pension paid in respect of disability, pregnancy, injury or sickness
- Any period for which you held a state studentship or comparable award
- Any period during which you could not support yourself because you had to look after a person under 18 who is wholly or mainly financially dependent on you.

Household contribution scales 2004/5

Once all the relevant income of the household has been assessed, the relevant amounts are added together to give the total household income. The following table gives an indication of the contribution expected at various levels of income (except in the case of single, independent students – for that contribution scale, see page 37).

Household income £	Rate of contribution £	Household income £	Rate of contribution £
less than £21,475	no contribution	28,000	731
21,475	45	29,000	837
21,493	47	30,000	942
22,000	100	35,000	1,468
23,000	205	40,000	1,995
24,000	310	45,000	2,521
25,000	416	50,000	3,047
26,000	521	55,000	3,573
27,000	626	88,260	7,075
			(maximum contribution)

So your household (often your parents) is assessed for the level of contribution it will make to your overall financial support. When allocating that support, the first port of call is tuition fees:

- Household income less than £21,475 – full grant for tuition fees
- Household income of between £21,475 and £31,972 – partial grant for tuition fees
- Household income of £31,973 or more – no grant for tuition fees.

Any remaining contribution assessed would go towards living costs. First, towards any grants for dependants, if appropriate. Then towards the means-tested element of the student loan.

Single independent student contribution scales

This income scale applies only if you are classed as an independent student (see page 34) and you do not live with a husband, wife or cohabiting partner of the opposite sex.

Student's income £	Assessed rate of contribution £	Student's income £	Assessed rate of contribution £
Below 10,000	no contribution	24,000	1,518
10,000	45	25,000	1,623
10,018	47	30,000	2,150
12,000	255	35,000	2,676
14,000	466	40,000	3,202
16,000	676	45,000	3,729
18,000	887	50,000	4,255
20,000	1,097	55,000	4,781
22,000	1,308	76,785	7,075
			(maximum contribution)

Again, your income is assessed for the overall contribution you will make to your education. When allocating support, the first port of call is tuition fees, at the following thresholds:

- Income of less than £10,000 – full grant for tuition fees
- Income of between £10,000 and £20,925 – partial grant for tuition fees
- Residual family income of £20,926 or more – no grant for tuition fees.

Any remaining contribution assessed would go towards living costs: firstly towards any grants for dependants, if appropriate; then towards the means-tested element of the student loan.

Examples

Look, we know it's a complex situation so, like all the best maths books, here are a few examples which might make it clearer:

■ The Applebys

Mr and Mrs Appleby have two children and live in London. Their son Humphrey is entering the second year of his degree course in October 2004, while his sister is still at secondary school.

Assessed household income

Humphrey's expected taxable income (not including part-time work) for the 2004/5 academic year	£500
Mr and Mrs Appleby's joint gross income for the tax year 2003/4	£34,000
Payments to pension schemes that attract tax relief	£1,500
Disregard for dependent child	£1,000
Total assessed income	£32,000

■ The Robertsons

Zoe Robertson is about to start a course in October 2004. She lives with her mother Angela and Angela's partner Dave.

Assessed household income

Zoë's expected taxable income (not including part-time work) for the 2004/5 academic year	£0
Angela and Dave's gross income for the tax year 2003/4	£22,000
Payments to pension schemes that attract tax relief	£800
Total assessed income	£21,200

■ Zarashpe

Zarashpe is 34 and lives with his partner Elizabeth. He is starting a course in October 2004.

Assessed household income

Zarashpe's expected taxable income (not including part-time work) for the 2004/5 academic year	£0
Elizabeth's gross income for the tax year 2003/4	£17,000
Total assessed income	£17,000

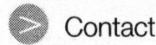 Contact

- **Department for Education and Skills (DfES)**

  (t) 0870 000 2288
  (Freephone Order Number: 0800 731 9133)
  Minicom: 0845 6055560
  Textphone: 01928 794 274

  (↗) www.dfes.gov.uk

- **Student Loans Company Ltd**
  100 Bothwell Street, Glasgow G2 7JD

  (t) 0800 40 50 10 (freephone)
  Minicom: 0800 085 3950

  (f) 0141 306 2005

  (↗) www.slc.co.uk

- **SKILL (National Bureau for Students with Disabilities)**
  Chapter House, 18–20 Crucifix Lane, London SE1 3JW

  (t) 020 7450 0620
  Information Service: 0800 328 5050 and 020 7657 2337
  Minicom: 0800 068 2422

  (e) info@skill.org.uk

  (↗) www.skill.org.uk

- **Mature Students' Union (UK)**
  21 Ambler Thorn, Queensbury, Bradford, BD13 2NP

  (t) 01274 881210

  (e) info@msu.org.uk

3 Student loans and repayments

Student loans are one of the most contentious aspects of the whole student financial package, and you'll also be living with this bit for the longest, as the 'loan' word is quite important. Once you've started work, your student loan will return to haunt you as, assuming you earn over the repayment threshold, you start to pay it back.

Though it seems rather daunting, the application process is actually pretty simple and forms part of the whole student support package. The loan, the tuition fee support and the grant are all part of the same process.

■ If your home is in England or Wales

As soon as you have a realistic prospect of attending an eligible course in full-time higher education, you should contact your LEA to ask for an **application form**. Ideally, this is done in March – you're dealing with people in local government, so it pays to be ahead of the game. You can also apply on-line at **www.studentfinancedirect.co.uk**. Remember to indicate whether or not you want a loan in the support request section.

Once your LEA has decided that you are eligible for financial support (see pages 12–13 for the criteria) and have assessed your household income, fill in that form and return it to your LEA, who will then let you know how much, if anything, you have to contribute to fees and the maximum amount of help with living costs you can apply for. This is shown on a **financial notice**, a copy of which is also sent to the **Student Loans Company (SLC)**.

Assuming you wish to continue with your application for a loan (and we advise you to do so if you think you will definitely have to borrow to support yourself as the student loan has a lower rate of interest and you won't pay it back until you are working), you should then complete the back of the financial notice (the **Loan Request form**) and send it to the SLC – address below.

The SLC then sets up the documentation for a loan account, makes the arrangements for the loan instalments and also arranges the payment of any tuition fees grant directly to the university or college.

The loan itself is usually paid in three instalments. The first instalment of student support will normally be paid by direct electronic transfer via the Bankers Automated Clearing System (BACS) into your bank or building society account. (A few students will have to collect a cheque at the start of the academic year.) The second and third instalments are paid by BACS at the beginning of subsequent terms.

If you want your loan to be available at the start of term, you must return your application form to your LEA by the end of May for continuing students and by the end of June for new students. If you're the tardy sort, you must still make your loan application within nine months of the start of the academic year. However, in certain circumstances the LEA can extend this limit.

■ If your home is in Scotland

The Scottish Executive has put in place a separate package of grants and awards, applicable to students whose home base is in Scotland. The Graduate Endowment Scheme is exclusive to Scotland and it provides for an entirely different approach. No Scottish domiciled student will pay fees 'up front', but a fixed amount is to be paid after graduation.

Application for funding is made to the Student Awards Agency for Scotland (SAAS). Instructions on loan payment amounts are sent to the Student Loans Company, who will normally make payments by BACS transfer at the start of each term. (A few students will still receive the first instalment by cheque, which they will pick up at their place of study at the start of term.) New applicants should submit their form as soon as they have even a conditional offer.

You have nine months from the beginning of the academic year to get your forms in to the SAAS.

■ If your home is in Northern Ireland

The process for Northern Irish students is exactly the same as for England and Wales, except that application is made to the local Education and Library Board (ELB) and application forms should be returned to the relevant ELB within four months of the start of the academic year.

For example, if your course starts in autumn 2003, you have until 31 December 2003 to apply. Once again, though, ELBs can, in certain circumstances, extend this four-month time limit.

■ What you'll get

The student loan has two elements – **means-tested** and **non-means-tested**.

As you should have picked up by now, the income assessment process is the same as for the tuition fees grant. But with 75 per cent of the loan non-means-tested, even the wealthiest among you should qualify for the cash. If you're in Scotland or Northern Ireland, see pages 51–3 and pages 58–9 for details of how the loans system works there.

As with other student funding, it is divided up into 'London', 'outside London' and 'living with your parents'. It's also different in your final year; but don't fret, you'll be earning soon. The rates for 2004 will be:

Full Year Rates	Maximum available	75 per cent (for all)	25 per cent (means-tested)
Students living away from home, studying in London	£5,050	£3,790	£1,260
NHS students living away from home, studying in London	£2,480	not relevant	not relevant
Students living away from home, studying elsewhere	£4,095	£3,070	£1,025
NHS students living away from home, studying elsewhere	£2,005	not relevant	not relevant
Students living at parent's home	£1,535	£2,430	£810
NHS students living at parent's home	£1,535	not relevant	not relevant

Final year rates	Maximum available	75 per cent (for all)	25 per cent (means-tested)
Students living away from home, studying in London	£4,380	£3,285	£1,095
NHS students living away from home, studying in London	£1,810	not relevant	not relevant
Students living away from home, studying elsewhere	£3,555	£2,665	£890
NHS students living away from home, studying elsewhere	£1,465	not relevant	not relevant
Students living at parents' home	£2,830	£2,125	£705
NHS students living at parents' home	£1,125	not relevant	not relevant

If you study abroad for eight or more weeks in a row as a necessary part of your course, you may be eligible for a higher rate of loan. This will depend on the country where you study. Your LEA will be able to tell you whether or not the higher rate of loan applies to your chosen country in 2004/5, when the maximum loan for study overseas will be £5,000 (£4,350 if you study abroad during the final year of your course).

If your course is longer than normal, you can get an extra amount of income-assessed loan to cover each extra week you have to be on your course above 30 term-time weeks (plus the short holidays) and for 45 weeks study or more in any 12-month period, you get an amount equivalent to 52 weeks. Maximum loan rate for each week = £94 in London; £73 outside London; £49 in parental home.

You do not need to make a separate application for this extra loan. It will be added by the LEA using information they will get about your course from your university.

■ Repayments

Repayment of student loans **begins in the April after you graduate** (or otherwise leave your course) and payments are taken from your salary by the Inland Revenue before it is paid into your bank account (except in the case of the self-employed, who will arrange repayment during the self-assessment process). However, payments are only taken if your income is above £10,000 per annum (this will increase to £15,000 per annum from April 2005), at a rate of 9 per cent of any income above this level. Payments continue until either the loan is paid off or your liability for repayment ceases because you have reached the age of 65; you become permanently unfit to work due to a disability; you die (great news!); or (in England only) you have not paid any remaining amount after 25 years.

If you intend to leave the UK after graduation or leaving your course, you should contact the SLC and make arrangements either to defer (via a third party with power of attorney) or begin repayment. If no arrangement is made, the SLC will attempt to trace you and request proof of earnings.

■ Complaining to the SLC

First, some basic rules about complaining. They apply to almost any organisation, as well as the SLC.

If you run into problems with the SLC, make sure you **keep clear records of all contact** with them, including details of all conversations, statements and agreements by both you and them, together with the name of the staff member contacted. If you make agreements on the phone, get them to acknowledge those agreements in writing as soon as possible. Make sure you deal with all correspondence from the SLC as quickly as possible.

You should also always **inform the SLC in writing of any changes in circumstances and address** and ask for this correspondence to be acknowledged in writing by them. If you do not hear from the SLC in a reasonable period of time, you should contact them to ensure that your letter was received.

Remember that the SLC now record phone calls. Not only does this mean that you should refrain from personal abuse, but it should also enable them to refer back to any phone call made within a reasonable period of time.

But before you start on a rant at the SLC for the fact that you don't get the means-tested element of the loan or your course isn't deemed eligible, remember that the actual decision about a student loan will be initially assessed by your LEA, ELB or the SAAS. The SLC is merely the paying agent for the loan and cannot be involved in appeals based on eligibility. It is the responsibility of the LEA, ELB or the SAAS to provide an appropriate appeals procedure.

But if you have complaints about the way the loan gets to you (or doesn't get to you) or the way it has been administered, then the SLC has a statutory obligation to deal with complaints from borrowers or intending borrowers in respect of their role in administering loans – for example, refusal to supply a loan, refusal to agree a deferment and disputes over the general administration of an intended borrower's application for a loan or a borrower's account.

To invoke the internal disputes procedure, a complaint should, in the first instance, be made in writing to:

> The Customer Services Manager, Student Loans Company Limited
> 100 Bothwell Street, Glasgow G2 7JD

The SLC aims to respond to all complaints within three days or, where this is not possible, to at least acknowledge the complaint and respond within 14 working days.

If you continue to be dissatisfied with the response, the complaint can move up each layer of SLC management until it reaches the chief executive.

If the SLC does not reach a decision on your complaint within three months or if you remain unsatisfied with the response from the chief executive, the matter may be referred to the Independent Assessor. This position is appointed by the SLC with the approval of the Secretary of State for Education and Skills and has wide powers to investigate any complaints referred to them. You should write to the SLC stating that you wish to have your case referred to the Independent Assessor, but first you must have gone through the full internal procedure.

The full complaints procedure is available online at: **www.slc.co.uk/ frames/corpinfo/complaints.htm**

The role of the Independent Assessor is to investigate and report on disputes referred to them between borrowers or intending borrowers and the SLC. They do not have a remit to investigate complaints in respect of a college's or an awards body's role in certifying eligibility.

The Independent Assessor may investigate a complaint if it constitutes:

- **a breach of the SLC's obligations** under any loans contract
- **unfair treatment**
- **maladministration** and this has caused you pecuniary loss or expense or an unreasonable degree of inconvenience.

The Independent Assessor will consider only written evidence submitted by you and the SLC. The Assessor will then produce a report, which will be sent both to you and the SLC.

If the Assessor makes recommendations to the SLC and you accept them (in writing) within three months, the SLC must either implement those recommendations or explain in its annual report to the Secretary of State for Education and Skills the reasons why they have not done so.

One of the recommendations the Assessor may make is that the SLC award compensation up to a maximum of £5,000 for any loss, expense, anxiety or inconvenience incurred by you.

Complaints about the administration of repayments by the Inland Revenue should at first be addressed to the IR internal procedures. If you are not satisfied with the outcome, an independent review of the case can be requested of the Inland Revenue's Adjudicator. Appeals against decisions by the Inland Revenue (for example, the amount of loan instalment due to be paid) should be addressed to the Tax Commissioners.

If you want to complain about the interest rate on the repayments, then try the government.

■ If you fall into arrears with the SLC

Well, frankly, you'll find it rather difficult, as the Inland Revenue controls repayments through the taxation system.

However, if you do not provide accurate information on your income to the Inland Revenue or if your liability for repayment is made under the self-assessment process and you do not make the repayments for which you are assessed, you may be charged additional interest and surcharges.

If you continue to fail to make repayments, the SLC may attempt to gain a court order.

■ Investing your loan

There won't be many of you, but some of you will come from a background comfortable enough not to have to worry too hard about cash. You will get by quite happily on the money you just happen to have lying around the family pile. So it seems odd to suggest even to you Lord and Lady Fauntleroys to take up the student loan, even if you don't need it – and take as long as possible to pay it off.

The idea is that because the Government has promised that interest on loans taken out to cover increased fees will rise only with inflation, you can invest it (carefully) and earn a bit of extra on the side. If you are 18 by the time you start the course you are entitled to invest in an Isa – up to £7,000 in a tax year at current rates (this will drop to £5,000 in the 2006/7 tax year).

You will only need to make repayments once you are earning more than £10,000 a year, at which point 9 per cent of your gross salary above that threshold will be automatically deducted for repayments. There would be little point in paying it off faster than that, because the Isa should be earning a higher rate of return in the meantime.

This is hardly what the Government had in mind by offering low-interest student loans, but it is a loophole that students from wealthier families could exploit. Since 25 per cent of student loans are means-tested, the remaining 75 per cent can effectively be a cheap source of investment cash for, ironically, wealthier students.

 Contact

■ **Student Loans Company**
100 Bothwell Street, Glasgow G2 7JD

General questions:
(t) 0800 40 50 10
Minicom: 0800 085 3950

(f) 0141 306 2005

**Questions about
your loan account:**
(t) For General Enquiries:
0870 24 222 11

(t) For Deferment Enquiries:
0870 60 60 70 4
Minicom: 0870 241 4632

**If you are in arrears with
your loan repayments:**
(t) 0870 24 23 22 0
Minicom: 0870 241 4634

Disabled Helpline
(t) S Tel: 0870 60 60 70 4

■ A booklet, Student Loans: Guidance on Terms and Conditions, is available from the Department for Education and Skills (DfES) website:
(↗) www.dfes.gov.uk/studentsupport

Inland Revenue
(↗) www.inlandrevenue.gov.uk
/students

4 Scotland and Scottish undergraduates

■ You're Scottish and you study in Scotland

The financial support for Scottish students studying in Scotland (and for that matter studying in the rest of the UK) is processed by the **Student Awards Agency Scotland (SAAS)**.

There are currently **three systems of financial support** (who said this was going to be simple?):

1 for students who began studying in 1997/8 or earlier
2 for those who began studying in 1998, 1999 or 2000
3 and for those who began studying before 2001 or later.

For the purposes of simplifying a complex situation – and in the belief that if you began studying in 1998 you know the ropes already – we're going to concentrate on the last group. The rest of you can ask your local NUS representative or approach the SAAS for details.

No matter when you began your higher education, the residency conditions still apply: you must have been resident in the UK for the three years preceding the 'relevant date' at the beginning of your course. This date is either 1 August, 1 January, 1 April or 1 July, depending on when your course starts.

For example, the relevant date if you start your course in October 2004 is 1 August 2004; whereas if your course starts in January 2005 it would be 1 January 2005. It's the nearest preceding date, basically.

And if you want to apply for support from the SAAS, then you must also be a resident of Scotland on that date. That's resident, not holiday-maker, so if you have doubts about your residency, contact the SAAS and they'll tell you how you stand.

To apply for support from the SAAS you must also be ordinarily resident in Scotland on that date. If you have any queries about your residency, contact the SAAS for guidance.

Tuition fees

The good news for Scottish students is that your tuition fees will be paid in full by the SAAS, once they approve the eligibility of you and your course, so long as you successfully complete the form. This is not dependent on any income assessment or means test. The form is available on the SAAS website or you can contact them direct:

The Student Awards Agency for Scotland
Gyleview House, 3 Redheughs Rigg, Edinburgh EH12 9HH

(t) 0845 111 1711 (8.30 a.m.–5 p.m.)

(f) 0131 244 5887

(e) saas.geu@scotland.gsi.gov.uk

(↗) www.saas.gov.uk

The catch for having your fees paid for you with such apparent ease and efficiency is that you may have to pay back a **graduate endowment** at the end of your studies. Towards the end of your third year, you will receive a letter from the SAAS explaining how much you have to pay and the options for doing so.

The amount payable depends on the year in which you began your studies (as it rises with inflation each year). But the table below gives you an idea of what you can expect.

Year of entry	Amount payable
2001/2	£2,000
2002/3	£2,030
2003/4	£2,092
2004/5	TBA

Not all students will be required to pay the endowment. You will not have to if you are assessed as 'independent' at the beginning of your course; if you receive the lone parents' grant or disabled students' allowance; if you are given an NHS bursary; if you are studying for an HNC or HND only (or then go on to no more than one year of a degree course); or if you study outside Scotland.

If you are studying for a second degree, are a part-time student and/or fail to meet the requirements for a degree, you will also be exempt.

Payment of the endowment will be due the April following your graduation. You have the choice of paying it in full at that point or you can take out a specially arranged student loan for part of or the entire amount. The loan will then be repaid under the standard loan system.

Loans and bursaries

The options for getting money to actually survive on for Scottish students in Scotland is based on the loans system and on one of two bursaries. You can apply for the **Young Students' Bursary** or the **Mature Students' Bursary**, but not both. You can't be young and mature, let's face it.

Young Students' Bursary

The Young Students' Bursary is a non-repayable means-tested grant of up to £2,150 a year. You can qualify if you are single, dependent on your parents (i.e., you have no significant personal income) and are under 25 at the beginning of your course.

The bursary is paid instead of part of the student loan, thereby reducing the amount that you are required to borrow. The full amount will be available if your parents' income is under £10,740; then a reduced amount is available on a sliding scale, which tapers to zero if your parents have an income of more than £27,900.

You are eligible for the bursary if:

☑ You are eligible for help with your tuition fees

☑ You are a new student, your course started in 2001/2 or later, or you returned to your studies in 2001/2 or later after a break of a year or more

☑ You are a Scottish resident and you are studying in Scotland

☑ You are or were under 25 before the first day of the first academic year of your course

☑ You were not married on the first day of the first academic year of your course

☑ You have not supported yourself from your earnings or benefits for any three years before the first day of the first academic year of your course

☑ You are taking a full-time course of higher education (HNC, HND, degree or an equivalent course) or a PGCE or PGDipCE course following a break of study of one year or more after completing your degree.

Mature Students' Bursary

The Mature Students' Bursary is run by colleges and universities, rather than the SAAS, so you need to apply to the institution you're studying at if you want the cash.

They are offered on a discretionary basis and are aimed at helping mature students with the extra costs of being a grown-up – particularly childcare, but also housing and excess travel costs. In 2003/4 the maximum permissible grant was £2,000; the maximum amount for 2004/5 is under review at the time of going to press.

You can be eligible if:

- ☑ You are a UK resident
- ☑ You are studying at a publicly funded institution in Scotland
- ☑ Your course started in 2001/2 or later, or you returned to your studies in 2001/2 or later after a break in study of a year or more
- ☑ You have taken out your full student-loan entitlement
- ☑ You were 25 or over on the first day of the first academic year of your course
- ☑ You were married by the first day of the first academic year of your course
- ☑ You have been supporting yourself from your earnings or benefits for any three years before the first day of the first academic year of your course.

Student loans

The student loans system is not very different to that elsewhere in the UK, but we'll step through the application process briefly, to save you flicking through the book and breaking the spine.

You apply through the SAAS at the same time as you apply for support with your tuition fees and any grants you may be entitled to, but you can apply later if necessary.

You can apply for the total amount you are entitled to or a smaller amount. If you want, you can just apply for the non income-assessed amount (approximately 20 per cent of the maximum applicable rate), in which case your parents or husband/wife will not need to supply details of their income. You can make top-up applications during the academic year if you did not take out your full entitlement. You can do this by contacting the Student Loans Company (SLC).

Once your application has gone in, the SAAS will assess your entitlement through the income assessment part of the form. They will send you an **entitlement notice** and send the information to the SLC who will set up your loan account and send you a **loan payment schedule** (usually one payment per term) and details of how it will arrive – either sent to your institution or sent directly by BACS transfer to your bank account.

It is important that you keep all the documents you receive. You will need them to collect the first instalment of any money due to you. Once you have confirmation of your award, you will need to send all questions about the loan to:

The Student Loans Company Ltd
100 Bothwell Street, Glasgow G2 7JD

(t) **0800 405010** (freephone)

(↗) www.slc.co.uk

If you are eligible for the Young Students' Bursary you may also be entitled to apply for an additional loan of up to £530 a year, depending on the level of your family's income.

■ You're Scottish and you're studying elsewhere in the UK

As with undergraduate student support for those studying within Scotland, support for undergraduate students studying elsewhere in the UK varies depending on the year of entry on to the course. And as with the section above, we're going to ignore those of you who've already done a tour of duty and concentrate on those starting their courses more recently; that is, students who started a course in 2002 or later.

Tuition fees

The bad news is that Scottish students studying outside Scotland are treated on broadly the same basis as their English and Welsh counterparts. Tuition fees are set at £1,150 and you may be liable for all or part of this amount depending on your own income and that of your parents or spouse where appropriate. If you have a low family income, some or all of your fees may paid by the SAAS. The system works in the same way as you'll find on page 19, you just apply to the SAAS, rather than an LEA.

Student loans

The loans available work in the same way as for student loans in the rest of the UK. An element is means-tested and subject to your or your household's income and an element is available whatever your income. See page 20 for details but note that for Scottish students the income-assessed part of the loan is a higher amount.

Young Students' Outside Scotland Bursary

This is only available to young Scottish students outside Scotland. Most school leavers will be classed as 'young' and even if you haven't left school recently, you may be eligible for this bursary if you meet the following criteria:

- ☑ You are eligible for help with your tuition fees
- ☑ You are a new student, your course started in 2002/3 or you are returning to your studies in 2004/5 after a break of a year or more
- ☑ You are a Scottish resident and you are studying outside Scotland
- ☑ You are under 25 before the first day of the first academic year of your course
- ☑ You are not married on the first day of the first academic year of your course
- ☑ You have not supported yourself from your earnings or benefits for any three years before the first day of the first academic year of your course
- ☑ You are taking a full-time course of higher education (a HNC, a HND, a degree or equivalent course) or you are taking a Postgraduate Certificate in Education (PGCE) or Postgraduate Diploma in Community Education (PGDipCE) course following a break of study of one year or more after completing your degree.

The bursary is paid on top of any loan you are entitled to, and the amount depends on your family income. The top level is £530 a year if your family income is £16,110 or less a year; down to £215 a year for a family income of £18,000 and then down to zero.

If you are eligible for the Young Students' Outside Scotland Bursary and you get married during your course, you will continue to be eligible to receive the bursary. From the academic year following the date of your marriage, the amount of Young Students' Outside Scotland Bursary you receive will depend on your husband's or wife's income rather than your parents' income.

■ You're not Scottish, but you're studying in Scotland

Tuition fees

If you are an undergraduate student funded by a UK award body outside Scotland (an LEA or the Library Board in Northern Ireland) and are studying a traditional four-year honours course at a Scottish university, you will continue to be assessed to pay tuition fees for the first three years as you would in other UK institutions.

However, you will not have to contribute to the fourth year of your tuition fees, but instead should apply to the SAAS, who will pay the fees for you.

Loans, grants and bursaries

The financial support for maintenance is the same as that provided to students from England, Wales and Northern Ireland studying elsewhere in the UK. See page 9 for details.

■ You're an EU student studying in Scotland

If you are an undergraduate EU student studying at a Scottish institution, you will have your tuition fees paid for you by the SAAS, so you need to contact them at the address above. There are, however, no statutory provisions to help support your living costs while studying in Scotland. You're on your own or looking to your own country's educational provisions.

■ Healthcare students in Scotland

If you are studying a course in nursing, midwifery or the allied health professions you are eligible for a means-tested Scottish Health Department Bursary, as well as a student loan and other allowances.

The rates for the bursary in 2004/5 are:

- £1,655 if you live with your parents
- £2,170 if you live away from your parents' home
- £2,675 if you undertake your course in London.

The amount you receive will depend on your income and, where appropriate, that of your parents or spouse.

The rates for the student loan in 2004/5 are:

- £1,535 if you live with your parents
- £2,005 if you live in away from your parents' home
- £2,480 if you undertake your course in London.

The loan is not means-tested.

You may also be able to claim extra allowances if your course lasts longer than 30 weeks and three days, and if you have placement expenses. Speak to the SAAS, your students' association or NUS Scotland for more details.

■ Travel expenses

Undergraduate and postgraduate students funded by the SAAS are able to claim travelling expenses for daily travel between their term-time residence and the place of study and (if you don't live in the family home in term time, but are financially dependent on your parents) three return trips to the parental home.

The claims are subject to both distance and financial limitations, and it won't cover the full amount. The actual figures will be released by the SAAS later in the academic year.

Travel should be claimed separately on **form AB4**, usually available from institutions, students' associations and the SAAS from December, and this should be submitted to the SAAS by 31 January 2004 to receive the travel element with the third instalment of your support. The absolute deadline for applications for travelling expenses is 31 July 2005 for the 2004/5 academic year.

5 Northern Ireland and Northern Irish students

Student awards for Higher Education (HE) courses in Northern Ireland (and for Northern Irish students studying in Britain and Eire) are administered by the **Department of Employment and Learning (DELNI)**.

Applications for support are processed by five **Education and Library Boards (ELBs)**. You should apply to the ELB that covers the area in which you normally live, rather than where you intend to study. For contact details see page 227 in Appendix 1.

In order to receive support you will need to be resident in Northern Ireland at the time of application, and have been ordinarily resident in the UK for the three years immediately before the start of the academic year, although temporary absences for reasons of work or holiday are usually OK. If you are not certain if you are eligible for support, contact your ELB or NUS–USI for further guidance.

■ Tuition fees

Financial support for tuition fees is almost identical to that available in England and Wales (see pages 19–20 for details). Close readers of this book will know what to expect – exceptions. And you'd be right:

If you are a Northern Irish student attending a course at a publicly funded college in Eire, you will have your tuition fees paid by the Irish government. In addition, a registration charge of €670 (2003/4 rates) to cover exam and student services fees may be charged by the college, but you can claim this back from your ELB. Therefore it is important that you apply to your ELB to ensure any charge will be paid, even if you do not intend to apply for financial help towards living costs.

In addition, while the same general arrangements for contribution by your parents, spouse or partner towards the cost of tuition fees apply, the precise income thresholds for household contribution differ slightly in Northern Ireland. Briefly, this means your household must have an income of £35,287 in the last full tax year before a full contribution of £1,150 towards fees is expected. For further details of the means test see page 29, but please bear in mind the different income threshold.

■ Loans, grants and bursaries

Support for your living costs while attending university is available from a variety of sources.

Higher Education bursary

If you come from a low-income background, you may be eligible for a non-repayable, means-tested bursary of up to £2,000 to help with your living costs. The full amount is available if you have a household income of less than £10,250; whereas a partial amount is available on a sliding scale if your family's income is between £10,250 and £20,500. If you have a family income of more than £20,500 you are not eligible to receive the bursary.

Your bursary will be paid in three instalments over the course of the academic year, in the same way as the student loan.

Student loan

You can apply for a partially means-tested student loan to help cover living costs and other expenses, in the same way as in England and Wales and at the same rate although the means-tested element in Northern Ireland is £1,354 regardless of the rate of loan. But if you are entitled to the full rate of bursary (see above) the amount you can take in a loan is reduced by £1,500.

If you are entitled to a partial bursary, the rate of loan you can take out is reduced by the amount of the bursary you receive. You may be able to take out a higher loan if the length of your course exceeds 30 weeks plus any short holidays.

The Student Loans Company will pay your loan in three instalments, usually straight into your bank or building society account.

■ Students with dependants

If you have dependants you may be eligible for help through the Childcare Grant (see pages 22–3); the Parents' Learning Allowance (see pages 23–4); the Lone Parents Grant (see page 24); the Adult Dependants' Grant (see pages 24–5); the Disabled Students' Allowance (see page 25); and the Care Leavers' Grant (see page 26).

■ Teacher training

Students do not have to pay tuition fees for courses that lead to Qualified Teacher Status (QTS), such as a Postgraduate Certificate in Education (PGCE). If you are studying in England and Wales there are extra financial incentives, particularly in subjects experiencing teacher shortages, but these incentives are not available for courses in Northern Ireland.

■ Healthcare students

Northern Irish students who undertake degree courses in nursing, midwifery or an allied health profession (for example, physiotherapy, radiography, etc.) do not have to pay tuition fees. In addition, you are eligible for a means-tested bursary and a non-means-tested loan.

In 2004/5 the bursary rates are set at £2,040 if you live away from the parental home and £1,665 if you do not. Loans are set at £1,960 if you live in the parental home and £1,500 if you do not, unless you are in your final year, in which case the figures are £1,430 and £1,100 respectively.

If you are undertaking a government-funded nursing and midwifery diploma course in Northern Ireland you do not have to pay tuition fees. In addition, you are eligible for a non-repayable, non-means-tested bursary. In 2004/5 this is set at £5,360 a year if you are aged under 26 at the start of your course, and £6,035 a year if you are 26 or over.

You may also be eligible for additional allowances for dependants; payments to help with additional costs arising from a disability; plus expenses resulting from any placement you undertake. Contact the Bursary Administration Unit for more information.

6 Healthcare students

If you're a medical or dental student you're funded through the main undergraduate system like anyone else. However, **once you reach the fifth and sixth year of your course you become**, for the purposes of funding, a **healthcare student**. Note that if you're considering a career in medicine or dentistry and can't or don't want to start before 2006 and the introduction of top-up fees, the government announced in August 2004 that they will continue to pay your tuition in full for those last two years even if the university starts charging the full £3,000 (or indeed anything in between).

However, as that will inevitably be many years in the future, do make sure you check to make sure this is still the case nearer the time.

Non-medical healthcare students who have been accepted on National Health Service-funded places on full-time or part-time pre-registration courses in England may be entitled to financial support under the NHS Bursary Scheme. If you are studying in Wales, Scotland or Northern Ireland you should contact the appropriate awards agency for details of bursary support in those nations or check the Scottish and Northern Irish sections for brief summaries.

There are two types of bursaries: **means-tested** (see below) and (naturally enough) **non-means-tested** (see page 66), offered for different types of courses, but both bursaries include payment of tuition fees on your behalf.

■ **Means-tested bursary students**

The NHS bursary scheme will fund you if you are attending one of the following courses:

- NHS-funded places on Allied Health Professions (AHPs) courses, i.e., Chiropody, Dietetics, Occupational Therapy, Orthoptics, Physiotherapy, Prosthetics and Orthotics, Radiography, Speech and Language Therapy, and Audiology – provided the course has been recognised by either the British Association of Audiological Technicians (BAAT), the British Association of Audiological Scientists (BAAS) or the British Society of Hearing Therapists (BSHT)

- Pre-registration nursing and midwifery at degree level
- Professions complementary to Dentistry, i.e., Dental Auxiliary Courses, Dental Hygiene, Dental Therapy
- Nursing (including conversion courses for second level nurses).

Assuming you are on one of these courses and are personally eligible (see the personal eligibility criteria on page 12 for details), then you are eligible for a means-tested NHS bursary and a reduced rate, non-means-tested student loan.

Bursaries are paid in monthly instalments in advance. The initial payment is by cheque covering two months, sent to your college; the rest is paid by electronic transfer to your bank or building society account. Any necessary reimbursement of travel costs between clinical placement and your term-time residence is paid monthly in arrears.

The rates for the maintenance costs element of the bursary are as follows:

• Studying in London	£2,768
• Studying elsewhere	£2,253
• Living with your parents	£1,843

For attendance over 30 weeks and three days, additional allowances are paid at a weekly rate of:

• Studying in London	£94
• Studying elsewhere	£73
• Living at parental home	£49

Attendance over 45 weeks qualifies for 52 weeks' bursary and additional non means-tested disability-related costs.

Fees of £1,150 flat rate are paid to the institution on your behalf for eligible courses. This includes students from the European Union. EU students are not, however, eligible for maintenance support.

You may also be eligible for the following allowances and grants:

Dependants' allowances

These are means-tested allowances payable for any husband/wife, children or adult dependant who is wholly or mainly financially dependent on you. The income of these dependants is taken into account when determining whether you should receive this allowance.

- Spouse (or other adult dependant or first child if there is no spouse or adult dependants) £2,335
- Child aged under 11 £488
- Child aged 11–15 £977
- Child aged 16–17 £1,299
- Child aged 18+ £1,869

Single parents' allowance

Single students with a dependent child or children who are not cohabiting with another person are entitled to an additional supplementary grant of £1,153. However, this is not payable in addition to the Older Students' Allowance (i.e., you can choose to receive one or the other, but not both).

Two Homes Allowance

A Two Homes Allowance of £813 can be paid if you have dependants and must maintain a second home in addition to that where you live while attending the course.

Disabled Students' Allowance

If you are obliged to incur additional costs during your course as a consequence of a disability you may receive extra help from the NHS. See pages 25–6 for details.

Clinical placement costs

Any costs you incur as a result of clinical placements are reimbursed where appropriate, subject to means-testing. As well as the costs of public transport, it is possible to claim mileage allowances for using your own vehicle (car, motorbike or bicycle); costs associated with sharing a vehicle; parking costs; and certain accommodation costs.

Older Students' Allowance

If you have reached the age of 26 before the first day of the first year of your course, you are entitled to an additional allowance, depending on your age at the start of the course. The rates of allowances are:

Age at start of course	£
26	397
27	687
28	1,020
29 or over	1,348

As previously mentioned, this is not payable in addition to the Single Parents' Allowance and lone parents should select one or the other. Note that the Older Students' Allowance is only higher if you are aged at least 29 at the beginning of your course.

Care Leavers' Allowance

If you are under the age of 21 at the commencement of the course and, as a result of a court order, were in custody or care prior to attending your course, you are entitled to a maximum of £100 a week towards your accommodation costs, during the long vacation only.

Student loan

As a means-tested bursary holder, you are also eligible to apply for a reduced-rate student loan (this is not means-tested):

	Full Year	Final Year
Living away from home, studying in London	£2,480	£1,810
Living away from home, studying outside London	£2,005	£1,465
Living at parental home (London or elsewhere)	£1,535	£1,125

Repayment of the loan is dependent on your income. You pay 9 per cent of any earnings over £10,000 per annum. This level should rise to £15,000 from April 2005. See pages 44–5 for more details

Access to Learning Funds

Higher education institutions are allocated funds to provide help for home students in financial difficulty. See pages 87–9 for more details.

NHS hardship grant scheme

If you are on a full bursary and have exhausted all available sources of financial support, you may get additional help from the Hardship Grant Scheme.

Mature, postgraduate, part-time and disabled students are beneficiaries, especially if you have to commute long distances or have to honour previous, unavoidable financial commitments. The scheme is not intended to provide loans, advance payments of maintenance grants or support if you are a self-funding student.

For more information or to apply for the scheme you should contact your department, but note that Diploma and EU students cannot apply for this scheme.

Repeat study

It is possible for you to continue to receive funding if you are required to repeat any part of your course. However, you will need the agreement of the NHS to receive this funding. Contact your department for more information on this.

■ The means test

For details as to how the means test (or income assessment, to give it its posh name) works, see page 29. Note that for healthcare students there is a different scale for spouse/partner contributions, and there is a different system of disregards. Contact the NUS or the NHS Student Grants Unit if you need more details.

■ Where to apply

Only NHS-funded places qualify for NHS bursaries. When you have accepted an offer of an NHS-funded place, the college will supply the **NHS Student Grants Unit (SGU)** with your details.

The SGU will then send a bursary application pack, which you should complete and return. They will then assess your eligibility and level of bursary support and notify you of their decision by letter. To ensure that the first instalment of the bursary is paid at the start of your course, you should endeavour to return application forms to the SGU by 31 July.

Nursing or midwifery degree students should apply for an application package to UCAS.

Application for the student loan should be made to your LEA before the start of the course. Details of how to do this will be included in your bursary application pack.

■ Non-Means-Tested Bursary

If you are on a **nursing or midwifery diploma course (DiPHE)** or on a first level conversion course (from second to first level registration as a nurse), you are eligible for a non-means-tested bursary to cover 45 weeks of the academic year and the payment of your tuition fees – assuming, of course, that you pass the personal eligibility tests (see page 12).

You may also be eligible for means-tested Dependants' Allowances, an Older Students' Allowance and Care Leavers' Grant, and the reimbursement of travel costs.

The non-means-tested bursaries are paid at the following rates:

• Studying in London	£6,692
• Studying elsewhere	£5,695
• Living in the parental home	£5,695

If you have to move to London to attend a practice placement, your basic maintenance grant will be temporarily increased by £17 a week for the length of the placement.

■ How to apply

Once you've been accepted on to a NHS-funded place, the NHS Student Grants Unit will send you an application pack for the bursary. You should return this to them as soon as possible. Applications for places on a course should be made to the Nursing and Midwifery Admissions Service (NMAS).

■ There's also the chance of some other funding and allowances:

Dependants' Allowances

The Dependants' Allowances available to nursing or midwifery students are means-tested on your dependants' income. The general dependants' income disregard (i.e., the income they'll simply ignore when calculating what you can get) is £770 per annum.

Maximum allowances for dependants (adult, spouse or child):	
• Spouse (or other adult dependant or first child if there is no spouse or adult dependants)	£1,980
• Child aged under 11	£419
• Child aged 11–15	£833
• Child aged 16–17	£1,101
• Child aged 18 or over	£1,578

Single Parents' Allowance

Single parent students are entitled to an additional £977 a year. This is not payable in addition to the Older Students' Allowance (i.e., you can be paid one or the other, but not both).

Older Students' Allowance

All diploma students who are 26 or over at the start of their course are entitled to an additional allowance of £666. Graduates on accelerated programmes are also entitled to this, regardless of age.

Initial Expenses Allowance

You are entitled to an additional Initial Expenses Allowance of £55. This is a one-off payment made in the first year of your course.

Clinical Placement Costs

Costs incurred as a result of practice placements are reimbursed where appropriate. Check with your institution as to exactly what 'appropriate' means.

Care Leavers' Grant

A care-leaver student's allowance of £100 a week is paid during the long vacation. Identical eligibility criteria to means-tested bursary students apply (see page 26).

Disabled Students' Allowance

You can apply for a Disabled Students' Allowance on the same basis as degree students. See page 25 for more details.

Access to Learning Funds

You can also apply for these on the same basis as degree students. See page 87 for more details.

Childcare Allowance

From September 2004 NHS-funded healthcare students can apply for help with childcare costs. The new **Childcare Allowance** (**CCA**) is broadly similar to the support offered to undergraduates through the **Childcare Grant** (see page 22).

It is available if you have dependent children who are aged under 15 – or aged under 17 for children with special educational needs – on the first day of the academic year.

The childcare must be provided by a 'registered' or 'approved' childcare provider. The allowance pays up to 85 per cent of your childcare costs up to a maximum of £114.75 a week for one child or £170 a week for two or more children. The exact amount of support you receive will depend on your income, that of your dependants and your individual circumstances.

■ Career Development Loans

See page 86 for more details on Career Development Loans or call 0800 585 505 or visit the CDL website at **www.lifelonglearning.co.uk/cdl**.

■ Part-time students

If you are a part-time student on a NHS-funded AHP degree course, you are eligible for 75 per cent of the means-tested NHS bursary.

For students doing the nursery or midwifery diploma, the part-time non-means-tested bursary is calculated as the appropriate portion of full-time study. Any additional costs you have as a result of a disability, and any reimbursement of expenses incurred attending clinical placements, will be reimbursed in full.

■ Students of medicine and dentistry

The NHS bursary scheme also covers pre-registration students of medicine and dentistry, if you are personally eligible (see pages 61–2 and 66 for details).

If you are a graduate student and are domiciled in England and you are on a four-year graduate-entry medical course, you will be assessed under the main undergraduate support system during year one (see section 1). During years two, three and four you will be eligible for NHS bursaries, including fee support, a means-tested bursary and reduced-rate student loan.

If you are a pre-registration medical and dental student and resident in England, you will be assessed under the main undergraduate support system during years one to four. From year five of a medical or dental degree course you will have the tuition fees paid and will be eligible for NHS-funded means-tested bursaries as well as reduced-rate student loans (see section 2).

If you are a graduate and have joined the undergraduate course and are exempted from undertaking some years, you will become eligible for NHS funding from the fifth year of the course. For example, if you are allowed to enter the course at year two, then you will be eligible from year five of the course, which is year four of your period of study.

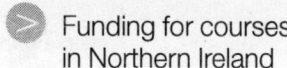

Funding for courses in England

- **NHS Student Grants Unit**
  22 Plymouth Road,
  Blackpool FY3 7JS
  - (t) 01253 655 655
  - (f) 01253 655 660
  - (e) nhs-sgu@ukonline.co.uk

- **Student Loans Company Ltd**
  100 Bothwell Street,
  Glasgow G2 7JD
  - (t) 0800 40 50 10 (freephone)
    Minicom: 0800 085 3950
  - (f) 0141 306 2005
  - (↗) www.slc.co.uk

- **Funding for courses in Wales**
  The NHS (Wales) Student Awards
  Unit, 2nd Floor, Golate House,
  101 St Mary Street,
  Cardiff CF10 1DX
  - (t) 02920 261 495

Funding for courses in Scotland

- **Student Awards Agency
  for Scotland**
  Gyleview House, 3 Redheughs Rigg,
  Edinburgh EH12 9HH
  - (t) 0845 111 1711
    (8.30 a.m.–5 p.m.)
  - (f) 0131 244 5887
  - (e) saas.geu@scotland.gsi.gov.uk
  - (↗) www.saas.gov.uk

Funding for courses in Northern Ireland

- Department for Health,
  Social Service and Public Safety,
  Bursary Administration Unit,
  Central Services Agency,
  25 Adelaide Street,
  Belfast BT2 8FH
  - (t) 028 9055 3661
  - (f) 028 9055 3689

General information

- **Free booklet available on request
  from**
  Department of Health Publications
  PO Box 777, London SE1 6XH
  - (t) 08701 555 455
  - (f) 01623 724524
  - (e) doh@prolog.uk.com

- **Applications for study should be
  made to:**
  UCAS (for degree-level study)
  - (t) UCAS 0870 1122211
  - (↗) www.ucas.com

  or

  NMAS (for diploma-level study)
  Rose Hill, New Barn Lane,
  Cheltenham, Glos GL52 3LZ
  - (t) NMAS 0870 1122206
  - (↗) www.nmas.ac.uk

- **NHS Careers Helpline**
  - (t) 0845 6060 655

7 Initial Teacher Training

The government would like you to become teachers. Not all of you, obviously, but enough to put some life back into the nation's schools. Hence, there's a whole series of incentives to get you back to the classroom that you may have just left.

■ Routes into Initial Teacher Training

There are three main routes for **Initial Teacher Training** (**ITT**) leading to **Qualified Teacher Status** (**QTS**), and the financial support is different for each, so just to check which one you are on:

Bachelor of Education (**BEd**): an undergraduate degree, usually for four years full-time study or equivalent, with QTS gained after a year's successful teaching

Postgraduate Certificate in Education (**PGCE**): a postgraduate degree, usually for one year or part-time equivalent, with QTS gained after a year's successful teaching. There is also the option of the fast-track programme designed to develop leadership skills within education

School-Centred Initial Teacher Training (**SCITT**). This can be undertaken through two routes:

- Registered Teacher Programme: up to two years of undergraduate degree study while training and working as a teacher to gain QTS

- Graduate Teacher Programme: up to one year of postgraduate training while working as a teacher to gain QTS.

■ BEd

Basic support

Students on full-time and part-time courses of ITT and who meet the personal criteria (section 1) are entitled to apply for the basic undergraduate student support package, i.e., a means-tested grant for tuition fees of up to £1,150; a Higher Education Grant of £1,000; and a means-tested student loan.

The maximum full-year loan rates in 2004/5 are £4,050 if you are living away from home and studying in London; £4,095 if you are living away from home and studying outside London; and £3,240 if you are living in your parents' home. Twenty-five per cent of the loan is means-tested.

Additional supplementary grants are available depending on your circumstances, such as the Welsh Assembly Learning Grant, the Childcare Grant and the Disabled Students' Allowance. See pages 22–7 for more on this.

Discretionary support

Besides the 'normal' undergraduate system, there's the safety net of discretionary support, including:

Access to Learning Funds

Each institution will have discretionary funding to address student financial hardship. BEd and PGCE students who meet the personal and residential criteria outlined above are eligible to apply (see pages 87–91).

Secondary Shortage Subject Scheme (SSSS) – England only

If you are on an undergraduate or postgraduate ITT course in England in one of the secondary shortage subjects (Maths, Science, Modern Languages, Design and Technology, Information Technology, Music and Religious Education) you are eligible to apply for support from the SSSS. If you are training within Key Stage 2 and 3 courses in these subjects you are also eligible.

Funds are available through your institution and assessment will be based on need. The maximum support available is £6,000 a year. Other forms of student support available will be taken into account. International students are eligible for this support.

Secondary Undergraduate Placement Grants (SUPG) – Wales only

A £1,000 grant is available to undergraduate teacher trainers in Wales who are studying one of the secondary shortage subject areas (Maths, Science, Modern Languages, Design and Technology, Information Technology, English [including Drama] and Welsh). If you are studying in non-shortage areas, £600 is payable. The grant will be paid through the teacher-training provider in two instalments during each year of the course.

Welsh Medium Incentive Supplement (WMIS) – Wales only

A £1,200 grant is available if you are an undergraduate or postgraduate students and undertaking a secondary ITT course in Wales using the Welsh language. The incentive is to help you if you 'need additional assistance to raise competence and confidence'.

Once qualified, you are expected to take up a teaching post using the Welsh language. Decisions concerning eligibility will be made by your education provider.

■ PGCE

If you are accepted on to a full- or part-time PGCE course and meet the usual eligibility criteria outlined (see page 12), you will be entitled to apply for the **HE grant**, a means-tested student loan and other supplementary grants such as the **Childcare Grant** and the **Disabled Students' Allowance**. What's more, PCGE students do not have to pay tuition fees.

- You are also eligible to apply for the Access to Learning Funds. See pages 87–91 for details.

■ Added incentives

Teacher training salary

A salary of £6,000 a year is available if you are undertaking a primary or secondary postgraduate ITT course and are not already employed as a teacher. Where your course lasts for one year you are paid in monthly instalments between October and June. If your course is part time the salary will be paid in instalments in accordance with the length of your training. Payments are made by the training provider.

- **If you are on a modular course** you are eligible as long as you are not already employed as a teacher in a school or within further or higher education. One payment of £3,000 is made after you have registered for the first assessment module, and the second is paid after you have qualified

- **For full-time trainees** the salary is not taxable and National Insurance contributions will not be paid. For part-time trainees, the salary may be taxable, depending on your total income for the year.

Fast Track programme

If you join the Fast-Track programme (a scheme which offers rapid career progression for those with at least a 2.1 degree) you receive a Fast-Track bursary of £5,000. One payment of £3,000 is made at the beginning of the PGCE and £2,000 is paid when you start your first Fast-Track teaching job, which must be within 15 months of qualification.

'Golden hello'

This is a £4,000 incentive if you train in certain shortage subject areas (Maths, Science, Modern Languages, Design and Technology, Information and Communication Technology, English [including Drama] or Welsh [in Wales]).

The money is paid if you have successfully qualified and are entering your second year of teaching, providing the second year is within twelve months of the induction year. The post must be within a school in England or Wales in the maintained sector, or a city technology college or a non-maintained special school or a primary school where you are responsible for teaching one or more of the shortage subjects to pupils other than your own class.

The position must also be permanent or on a fixed-term contract of more than a term's duration. The incentive will be paid in a lump sum with your salary. You will need to inform the school that you are eligible to receive the incentive. The payment is taxable.

■ Graduate Teacher Programme (GTP)

The GTP allows graduates aged 24 or over to train as a teacher in a maintained school while still earning a living.

If you start a GTP you receive a salary from the school in which you are based. The level of salary to be paid by the school will be agreed by the governing body, but it will be at least £13,266 (the lowest point on the unqualified teacher salary scale). Trainees on the GTP are not eligible for the £6,000 training salary or for the £4,000 'Golden Hello'.

The school receives £4,000 a year for the cost of your training. This can be used to cover the cost of your initial training needs assessment, tuition fees, supply cover, mentoring training, learning resources and materials, but it cannot be used as a wage supplement.

■ Registered Teacher Programme

This scheme is similar to the GTP, but allows those who have yet to complete the necessary degree-level qualification to study for this in addition to their teacher training within the maintained school. As with the GTP, the school pays you and receives £4,000 for your training to be used for the same purposes as the GTP. The only real difference is that your salary is not guaranteed by the scheme and can be below the £13,266 level.

■ Repayment of Teacher's Loans (RTL)

This is a pilot scheme for newly qualified teachers who have taken up or will take up a teaching post in the academic years 2002/3, 2003/4 or 2004/5. If you are eligible and you work in a shortage subject (see above) you will have your student loan repaid. The scheme only applies to teachers who spend at least half of their teaching time in a school week teaching the shortage subjects.

To be eligible you must:

☑ be employed in a teaching post at a maintained school, a non-maintained special school, a City Technology College, a City College for the Technology of Arts or a City Academy in England or Wales

☑ begin or have begun your employment between 1 July 2002 and 30 June 2005

☑ be employed to teach one or more of the shortage subjects for at least half of your teaching time within a normal school week.

More information is available at the Teachernet website at **www.teachernet.gov.uk/teachersloans**.

 Contact

- **Department for Education and Skills (DfES)**

  (t) 0870 000 2288
  Textphone: 01928 794 274
  Minicom: 0845 6055560
  Publications: 0800 731 9133

  (e) info@dfes.gsi.gov.uk

  (↗) www.dfes.gov.uk

  The booklet Financial Support for Higher Education Students in 2004/5 is available in print and on the website.

- **Teacher Training Agency**

  (t) 020 7925 3700 / 0845 6000 991
  Minicom: 01245 454 343

  (e) teaching@ttainfo.co.uk

  (↗) www.useyourheadteach.gov.uk

  For general information and details of the Graduate and Registered Teacher Programmes.

- **Teaching Information Line**

  (t) 0845 6000 991 for further details on teaching in England and Wales. There is also a Welsh language line on 0845 6000 992.

- **Fast Track Programme Information**

  (↗) www.fasttrackteaching.gov.uk

8 Part-time students

■ Tuition fees

As of September 2004 a new tuition fee grant of up to £575 is available if you are a part-time student studying at least 50 per cent of a full-time course. You and your course must meet the eligibility criteria, which are the same as for full-time student (see pages 12–13). As with full-time students, the grant is means-tested and you will have to pay any amount of tuition fee above the level of grant you are awarded yourself.

■ Means test

The means test is not very different to the process for full-time students. To qualify for full support (including the part-time course grant, see page 78) your income must have been less than £14,600 in the last full tax year.

If it is between £14,600 and £21,487 partial help will be available on a sliding scale. If your income should change by more than £1,000 from the previous tax year to the academic year in which you intend to study you can ask for a reassessment based on your current income.

In addition, £2,000 will be subtracted from your assessed total income **if you have a spouse or heterosexual partner**. Two thousand pounds will also be subtracted from this income for your eldest dependent child, with a further £1,000 subtracted for each additional dependent child.

If you are in receipt of income-assessed social security benefits you will automatically receive full support.

If the annual fee for your course is less than £575 you will not be awarded more than the actual cost of the fee, and you can apply for support for no more than eight years.

Application packs will be available from the DfES from late summer 2004. You can either contact their information line on 0800 731 9133 or visit the DfES website at **www.dfes.gov.uk/studentsupport**.

Part-time student course grant

A means-tested grant of up to £250 a year is available to new and existing students. You can be assessed for it at the same time as for your tuition fees grant. It's just a question of ticking the right boxes. The old-style part-time student loan is no longer available.

Disabled Students' Allowances for part-time students

If you qualify for part-time loans and you incur additional costs during your course due to a disability, you may apply to your LEA for help with these costs. The non-means-tested Disabled Students' Allowances (DSAs) are:

- **Non-medical helper** a percentage of the full-time rate (up to £11,550)
  For example: 50 per cent of a full-time course: up to £5,775
  60 per cent of the full-time course: up to £6,930
- **Specialist equipment** up to £4,565 for the duration of the course
- **Other expenditure** a percentage of the full-time rate (up to £1,525)
- **Extra travel expenditure** full reimbursement

In all other regards, the DSA is the same process for part-time students as for full-time, so see pages 25–6 for details or proof of disability and any extra costs.

Access to Learning Funds

Part-time undergraduates are eligible to apply for additional help from the discretionary Access to Learning Fund, providing your course is worth a minimum of 60 credits per academic year, where a full-time equivalent course is 120 credits, or otherwise at least 50 per cent of a full-time course. See pages 87–91 for more on the Access to Learning Fund.

■ Changing courses

Transferring courses

You can transfer to another designated part-time course on educational grounds and retain your eligibility for funding. In which case, your LEA will need to confirm that you remain eligible, so you will need to contact them and let them know what's happening.

Converting from full- to part-time study

If you switch from a full-time course to a part-time course you remain eligible for the full-time living-cost support (loan and grant) for the duration of the academic year in which you transferred, regardless of when you transferred and any extra time it will now require for you to complete your course. So you carry on until the end of the current academic year, but you don't take the loan money any further.

Your eligibility for fee support ends once you reach the end of the period it would have taken you to complete the full-time course. So if your part-time course will (presumably) take you longer to complete, you don't get the fee support to tide you over. Contact your LEA for guidance.

Conversion from part- to full-time study

If you change from a part-time course to a full-time course and become eligible for full-time undergraduate support, the part-time support will be disregarded in calculating your entitlement to a grant for tuition fees, loans and grants for living costs.

If you transfer during the first term, you will receive your full assessed student loan amount. If you transfer during the second term, you will be eligible for two thirds of your assessed annual support. If you transfer during the third term, you will be eligible for one third of your assessed annual support.

■ Part-time students in Scotland

Tuition fees

Most part-time students will have to pay tuition fees. However, a **fee waiver scheme** may operate at your institution if you are unemployed or on a low income. Contact your institution for details.

Part-time student loan

A **means-tested student loan** of £500 a year is available to new and existing students who meet the personal and course eligibility criteria. You must:

☑ be ordinarily resident in Scotland on the first day of the academic year of your course

☑ be under 50 at the start of the course or be between 50 and 54 and have satisfied the SAAS that you intend to take up employment immediately after your studies

☑ be regarded as an independent student by the SAAS (i.e., you are not parentally dependent)

☑ not already hold a degree qualification

☑ not be in breach of any previous student loan agreement.

If you are undertaking more than one part-time course you will only be eligible for support for one course. You will need to confirm with your institution that your course allows you to get a loan.

Means test

To qualify financially for the part-time loan, you must either:

☑ be in receipt of Income Support, Housing Benefit or Council Tax Benefit

or

☑ have an assessed gross income in the previous financial year of £13,000 or below (or £15,000 if you are married).

Your income from the previous financial year, along with the income of your spouse if you have one, will be assessed to determine your eligibility.

If you have a disability, you may also be able to get assistance with any extra costs the disability creates. Ask the SAAS or your students' association for more information.

■ Part-time students in Northern Ireland

Part-time undergraduate students in Northern Ireland, as with those in England and Wales, can now apply for a tuition fees grant of up to £575 and a course costs grant of up to £25, but if you are resident in Northern Ireland you should apply to DELNI for this support rather than the DfES.

■ Postgraduate support

Funding for **part-time postgraduate students** is essentially the same as for full-time postgraduates. See pages 107–15 for details.

■ Part-time study and benefits

It may be possible to study part-time while claiming **Jobseeker's Allowance (JSA)**, **Income Support (IS)** or **Incapacity Benefit (IB)**, if you satisfy the other conditions for these benefits

The first hurdle to crack is the definition of part time. From the point of view of claiming benefit, **you are classified as part-time** if you fulfil one of the following criteria:

☑ you are under 19 and spend 12 hours a week or less in non-advanced education

☑ your course is funded by the Learning and Skills Council (LSC) or the National Council for Education and Training in Wales and has a Learning Agreement stating that it is made up of 16 guided learning hours or less per week. Guided learning hours include all supervised study, for example, classes, lectures, tutorials and structured assessment periods. They do not include unstructured or unsupervised study time, for example, studying at home or in a library. If you are on such a course you should be given a Learning Agreement by your education provider which states the number of guided learning hours. The Employment Service should accept this as evidence of 'part-time' study

☑ the course is one of higher education and is not defined as a full-time course by the education institution.

■ Income Support

If you claim Income Support and wish to study on a part-time basis, provided your hours of study fall within the relevant definition, your benefit entitlements should not be affected.

■ Jobseeker's Allowance (JSA)

Once again, if you wish to study on a part-time basis you may be able to continue to claim JSA, as long as you meet the normal criteria for claiming, that is, you can be said to be actively looking for work. But if you are repeating any part of the course that you undertook while registered on a full-time basis, you will not be able to claim JSA while registered part-time. You must be willing to give up the course if you are offered a position which would clash with any classes. However, you may reasonably restrict the times of availablity for employment with the agreement of your Employment Service Office. Speak to them about the conditions.

If you are claiming the JSA and wish to undertake study you are required to inform your Job Centre Plus and will be required to complete a **student questionnaire**. The continuation of your claim will be assessed on this. The questionnaire is complex. You should consult an adviser, preferably based at the potential education institution, before completing it.

9 Alternative financial assistance

■ Educational charities and trusts

It is unlikely that a course lasting more than one year could be financed entirely by trust fund help. Educational charities and trusts are, however, in a position to provide extra help to students who may be without funding for part of their course or who, for various reasons, may need help over and above that provided by public funds.

You have not just stumbled on a gold mine, though. Educational charities and trusts often have specific, even unusual, terms of reference. They may be restricted to helping, for example, students studying a particular course or students from particular parts of the UK or world or for courses leading to particular professions.

What's more, you're unlikely to receive more than about £300 from any one charity and they tend to make one payment rather than recurring ones and they're often for particular items – for equipment or childcare.

Creating a hard-luck story is likely to be counterproductive, but charities are more sympathetic to students whose need for assistance results from sickness or unforeseen circumstances, rather than students who have mismanaged their money or who have started a course knowing they didn't have the money to finish it.

And you're also more likely to get funds if you're a first-time student. Postgraduates or those taking a second undergraduate course are less likely to win funding.

And one more thing: applications often take some time to process, so it is wise to apply for support well in advance of the course start date.

If you want to plough on, however, there are a number of publications listing the extra funding opportunities open to students:

- **The Educational Grants Directory**
  Published annually by the
  Directory of Social Change (DSC).

  (t) 020 7391 4800

  (↗) www.dsc.org.uk

  Also available by mail order from
  the DSC.

  (t) 08450 77 77 07

  (e) books@dsc.org.uk

- **A Guide to Grants for
  Individuals in Need**
  Published annually by the DSC
  (see above)

- **Directory of Grant-Making Trusts**
  Published annually by the DSC
  (see above)

- **Charities Digest**
  Published by Waterlow's
  Legal Publishing

  (t) 020 7549 8670

  (↗) www.waterlow.com

- **The Grants Register**
  Published annually by Palgrave
  Macmillan Publishers Ltd.
  This is particularly relevant to
  postgraduate student awards
  for both the UK and overseas.

  (↗) www.palgrave.com

- **Study Abroad**
  Published by the United Nations
  Educational Scientific and Cultural
  Organisation (UNESCO)

  (↗) www.upo.unesco.org

- **International Awards 2001+**
  Published by the Association of
  Commonwealth Universities (ACU)
  and available in most university
  libraries or British Council Offices.

  (↗) www.acu.ac.uk/yearbook
  /awards.html

- **Scholarships for Study in the
  USA and Canada**
  Published by Peterson's, this book
  includes details of scholarships and
  financial aid for international
  students (including those from the
  UK) wishing to study in North
  America.

  (↗) www.petersons.com

- **British and International Music
  Yearbook** and **British Music
  Education Yearbook**
  Both published by Rhinegold

  (↗) www.rhinegold.co.uk

Here are a few websites that might help:

⊘ **Scholarship Search** www.scholarship-search.org.uk

⊘ **Funderfinder** www.funderfinder.org.uk

If you're a genuine case in need, consult your LEA, students' union, careers service, Citizens Advice Bureau, town hall and local clergy, as they may know of small local trusts.

As well as awarding scholarships and prizes in specific subjects, colleges may have funds available for students in financial difficulties and unable to apply to the Access to Learning or Learner Support Funds, so always consult the college student services too.

For more advice on alternative sources of funding contact the **Educational Grants Advisory Service** (**EGAS**). Remember, though, that EGAS cannot help students from outside the European Economic Area or students wishing to study outside the UK.

Their advice line is open from 10 a.m.–12 p.m. and 2 p.m.–4 p.m. Mondays, Wednesdays and Fridays only.

- **Educational Grants Advisory Service (EGAS)**
  501–505 Kingsland Road, London E8 4AU

  ⓣ 020 7254 6251   ⊘ www.egas-online.org.uk

■ Sponsorships

The Sponsorship and Funding Directory lists scholarships and bursaries for courses. It is often available in libraries. For the purposes of tax, sponsorships are treated as scholarships, meaning that they are not taxable as long as they do 'no more than support a student during a period of study'. If you are required to work in a company or organisation and your sponsorship is part-payment for this, you should contact the Inland Revenue for appropriate guidance.

■ Study loans

There is a number of schemes to help (usually) vocational studies. Although these are very useful schemes, remember that they are loans, not grants. You'll be paying them back one day.

■ Career Development Loans

The Department for Education and Skills, in participation with three major banks (Barclays, the Co-operative, and the Royal Bank of Scotland) operates a deferred repayment loan system. Between £300 and £8,000 can be borrowed towards fees and other expenses for students on vocational full-time, part-time and distance-learning courses lasting up to two years (and up to one year's practical work experience if it is part of the course). Degree and postgraduate courses are included.

Throughout the period of study and up to one month after completing or leaving the course, the DfES will pay the interest on the loan. Repayments are fixed and can be spread between one and five years. If you are registered unemployed at the end of the first month of completing your course, you may apply to the bank for deferment of repayment for up to five months initially, and for two further extensions of six months each.

For further information call 0800 585 505 or visit the CDL website **www.lifelonglearning.co.uk/cdl/**.

■ Professional studies loan schemes

In addition, four of the major high street banks (HSBC, Barclays, NatWest and Lloyds TSB) offer professional studies loans.

Some schemes are specifically aimed at study within certain fields (for example, medicine, dentistry, law, veterinary science and architecture). However, some banks now offer loans for general vocational study. Loans up to £20,000 are available (£25,000 for law students); interest rates and repayment terms are variable. Contact a local branch or visit the website of any of the above banks for more information.

■ Business school loan scheme

The Association of MBAs runs this scheme in conjunction with the NatWest bank. It is available to those studying for a Masters in Business Administration (MBA) or equivalent, full-time, part-time or by distance learning.

For further information contact NatWest on freephone 0800 200 400 or visit the Association's website at **www.mbaworld.com**. Some individual business schools also have a loan scheme with the HSBC bank. Contact the school to see if they participate.

10 Access to Learning Funds

From September 2004 all Hardship Funds in universities become Access to Learning Funds and in some cases the method of application will change. The priorities of some funds will also change. So everything you thought you knew may have changed. Read on...

■ **Access to Learning Fund (ALF)**

The Access to Learning Fund comes from the college or university you study at and is discretionary, so you have to prove that you need it. It is geared to helping those groups of students or potential students who might otherwise not be in a position to go on to higher education.

As a result, certain categories of students are considered as particularly vulnerable and therefore given priority when the ALF is distributed. For full-time undergraduates these are:

- students with children (especially lone parents); mature students; students with disabilities; care leavers; students who are homeless or have come from the Foyer Federation; and students in their final year.

For part-time undergraduates and postgraduate students they are:

- students with children (especially lone parents); students with disabilities; and students who are self-funding (i.e., receive no government assistance).

If you are not in one of the priority groups you can still apply for assistance from the funds, but you will need to prove that you are in particular difficulty.

■ **Applications**

The ALF office at your university will have application forms. If you do not know where this office is, ask at the Registry or your student union.

When you make an application, you will need to take evidence of your financial situation such as bank statements and notifications of support from your LEA or other funding body. Your application may be judged either as a **standard** or **non-standard assessment**. See below for more.

You can apply more than once in an academic year, but your circumstances will have to have changed if your application is to be considered.

■ Standard awards

There are two main awards under the Access to Learning Fund: standard and non-standard awards. For full-time students, standard awards are for help with the general costs of living and study, such as rent, childcare, food and utility bills. If, for whatever reason, the income you have over the year will be less than your reasonable necessary expenditure then you can apply for help to fully or partially bridge this gap.

Income

Various types of income will be taken into account. Most support you receive from the government or any other funding agency (for example, the NHS or a research council) will be included. Exceptions include the HE Grant and the now-defunct Opportunity Bursary, if you receive either of these. Income-related benefits (such as Income Support and Housing Benefit) are also included, but some other benefits (such as Child Benefit) are disregarded.

Unless you are a part-time student, you will also have an **assumed income figure**. This is an amount the government believes all students studying at your level should be able to achieve through part-time work, as well as those benefits which effectively replace your income (such as Incapacity Benefit), and the 'income' from other sourcess such as a bank overdraft.

If you should earn more than this through part-time employment, the excess will not be included in your claim, but excess unearned income may be. If you do not actually earn this level of income through whatever means, it will still be 'assumed' when assessing your claim.

For **full-time undergraduates** this income is set at £1,500 a year unless you are in your final year in which case it is set at £500 (on the grounds that you'll be earning soon). For **postgraduates** this is set at £165 per week of your course if you are studying in London and £135 if you are not – unless you have children or cannot work due to a disability, in which case the figures are set at £135 and £110 respectively.

If you are a **part-time student** your actual income is used.

Expenditure

When your income is added together it is then placed against your expenditure to determine whether you have excess income or a shortfall. Your assessed expenditure is divided into two types: **variable expenditure** and some notional **fixed expenditure**.

The fixed expenditure is known as your Composite Living Costs (CLC). Your CLC is based on a range of necessary expenditure (for example, food, utility bills, insurance and so on). The exact amount used when calculating your expenditure will, obviously, depend on the make-up of your household and where in the country you live, so ask at the ALF office when you make an application.

However, some expenditure is regarded as 'variable' and you should put down the exact amount. This includes rent or mortgage payments, travel and childcare. Your institution may 'cap' any amount it considers unreasonably high (for example, if you choose to live in an expensive flat, for the purposes of your application they may 'cap' the rent at a lower amount on the basis that you could have chosen to live somewhere less expensive).

Payments

After determining what (if any) shortfall you have, your university will then decide what percentage of that shortfall it is able to pay you. If you are in a target group you are more likely to be paid 100 per cent of the shortfall, but all payments are dependent on the number of applications made to the funds and the amount of money your institution has to spend.

■ Non-standard awards

If you find yourself in financial difficulty due to an unexpected or exceptional cost (for example, an essential household appliance requires repair, a bereavement means you must make an expensive journey, and so on) then you can make a limited application to help pay for this. This will be considered as a non-standard award.

Students with disabilities who have extra costs associated with their disability that are not covered by the Disabled Students' Allowance (see pages 25–6 for details on that) can also use this type of award to help cover these costs. This may include the cost of a diagnosis to prove eligibility for the DSA if one has not been carried out.

Application procedures will vary from institution to institution. Speak to the ALF office or your student union for guidance in this instance.

Eligibility

To be eligible to apply for assistance from the ALF, you must fulfil the eligibility criteria:

☑ If you are an undergraduate, you must be studying a full or part-time higher education course, which can include NHS-funded healthcare courses, a sandwich course or periods of placement. You can also be intercalating (i.e., taking time away from the course) as long as you intend to return

☑ If you are a postgraduate student you must be on a full or part-time course. You are also eligible if you are writing up your thesis and not otherwise attending your university

☑ If you are a FE student attending an HE institution, you must be 16 or over.

In addition you must be classed as a **'home' student**. This means you must have been resident in the UK for the three years before the start of your course. However, if you are a citizen of Eire or a recognised refugee (or the spouse or child of a recognised refugee) you do not have to fulfil the three-year rule.

If you are an asylum seeker and have exceptional leave to enter or remain or humanitarian protection or discretionary leave, you must meet the three-year residency requirement in the same way as other students.

If you are an EEA or Swiss national (or their child or stepchild) and can establish migrant worker status in the UK, you are eligible for help from the ALF. You must, however, be resident within the European Economic Area (EEA) or Switzerland. For those who don't know (most of us), the EEA consists of the 25 member states of the European Union plus Norway, Iceland and Liechtenstein.

If you are studying a course accredited by another institution (for example, studying at a FE college, but the course is accredited by a separate university) you must approach the accrediting institution for ALF support, not the FE college. Check local arrangements for how this process is administered.

If you are a part-time student trying to claim, then remember that the definition of 'part-time course' for the purposes of ALF is a course worth a minimum of 60 credit points per academic year, where a full-time equivalent is 120 credits or otherwise 50 per cent of a full-time course or more.

There is no set amount you will get from the ALF, since it is distributed by individual universities, but the DfES lays down guidelines to ensure that awards are pretty much the same across the board.

The fund cannot be used to meet the costs of your tuition fees if you are a full-time undergraduate student or if your parents, spouse or partner refuse to pay assessed contributions to your support, but it can be used for tuition fees for part-time students if you received a fee waiver in the academic year starting 2003, if you are receiving the full grant for your fees and those fees are over £5,756, in which case you will receive the difference between £575 and the money you have to pay.

If you have no previous experience of higher education and are taking a taster module, which is the equivalent of 10–50 per cent of a full-time course, you may be able to get some help for any tuition fee payable. Speak to the ALF office for more information.

There is no unified appeals process if you don't get what you think you deserve from the ALF; so if you want to appeal, ask your NUS officer for advice.

■ Learner Support Funds (LSFs)

If you are between 16 and 19, are studying an FE course and have been treated as eligible for free tuition, then you can apply to the Learner Support Funds. If you are aged 19 or over you must be on an FE course and must fulfil the residency requirements as for the ALF (see page 90). If you're under 16, you cannot apply.

If you are an asylum seeker aged 16 and over and under 19 you may apply to FE funds for assistance, even if you have not yet been resident in the UK for three years

Having said that, there are certain groups that get priority when your college is considering doling out the LSFs: students who are economically or socially disadvantaged; students with disabilities; lone parents; young parents; care leavers; those attempting to learn English as a second or other language; those receiving social security benefits due to unemployment and/or a low income; and unwaged dependants of any of these.

And while it's up to the college to decide how to allocate the cash, they are advised by the DfES to bear in mind whether you have exhausted all the other possibilities for funding; whether it's better to give you cash payments or short-term loans; and whether to give you the cash or whether they should allocate the money to communal services.

■ Specific bursaries

Childcare bursaries

FE colleges have a ring-fenced section of their Learner Support Funds to allocate to childcare. If you have a dependent child or children under 16 (or under 17 if they have special needs) and are eligible for LSFs (see above) you can apply for up to £5,125 a year for each child. This is the maximum full-time rate; if you are a part-time student, any payment will be allocated on a pro-rata basis.

The childcare must be approved or accredited or meet the requirements of the Children's Act 1989 (where registered childcare is not available); although unapproved childcare may be funded for no more than two hours a day if approved childcare is unavailable.

Those aged under 19 and using approved or registered childcare should apply to the Care to Learn scheme for assistance (see page 120).

Residential bursaries

The LSC and the DfES have also established a system for paying residential support to students other than those attending the Residential Bursary Colleges. The pilot targets full-time FE students of all ages who need to undertake courses at level 3 or above or who have a particular employment-related learning need, and where LSC agree that no suitable provision is available locally. Contact the college for further information.

Education Maintenance Allowances (EMAs) and Adult Learning Grants (ALGs)

If you are in receipt of an Education Maintenance Allowance (EMA) (see pages 117–20) or an Adult Learning Grant (ALG) (see page 93) you can be given payments from the LSFs to meet additional needs. Payments from the LSFs will not affect your eligibility for EMAs or ALGs or the level of payment made for either.

All the colleges have different application procedures, so ask your union rep for advice as to how to find out if you are eligible and how to claim.

■ Discretionary funding and your benefits

It might not be a one-way street as far as funding goes, you know.

If you are in receipt of means-tested social security benefits (Income Support/Housing Benefit/Jobseekers Allowance), payments from the ALF or LSF are treated in the same way as voluntary payments.

If you can show that the payment is not for an everyday living expense (your beer money, for example), the payment will be completely disregarded; if not, it will be taken into account.

If a payment is made on a regular basis, it will be subject to a disregard of £20 per week (£10 per week if you are also eligible for a full-time student loan). Which means that they won't count £20 (or £10) a week of it when working out what you can claim.

Ask your college for a letter explaining what the payment is for and how it is paid so that the Job Centre Plus deals with it appropriately.

LSF childcare bursaries are disregarded by Income Support, JSA, Housing Benefit, Council Tax Benefit and Tax Credits.

For the purposes of NHS healthcare benefits, payments from the ALF or LSF are treated as for social security benefits.

Payments from the ALF and LSF are disregarded entirely when assessing tax credits claims.

11 European Union students

Hopefully you noticed, but on 1 May 2004 ten more nations joined the European Union (EU): Cyprus, the Czech Republic, Estonia, Hungary, Latvia, Lithuania, Malta, Poland, Slovakia and Slovenia. When this happened, citizens of these ten nations became eligible for all UK government support provided to EU students from September 2004, subject to the normal regulations.

What's more, students from those countries will be treated as if they had always been part of the EU and so continuing students from those countries get the same treatment as new students.

■ Undergraduates

If you are a national of an EU country (including Gibralter) and have been ordinarily resident in the EEA or Switzerland for the three years immediately preceding the first day of the academic year of your course, you can be granted home fee status. The first day of the academic year is defined as 1 September, 1 January, 1 April or 1 July, whichever is the closest to the start of your course.

Once you have **home fee status**, you get the same fees treatment as a UK student, which means that it will be means-tested in much the same way (see section 2). One difference is that students' loan income received under your own country's legislation is disregarded under the means test, similarly to the treatment of the student loan and the Career Development Loan for UK students.

If you have won a place at a university in England or Wales you should complete **form EU4(N)**. If you applied for university places through UCAS (the Universities and Colleges Admissions Service) you will be sent this form automatically. If you have a place in Scotland, contact the SAAS to arrange payment of your fees. Contact DELNI if you are studying in Northern Ireland.

If you have not applied through UCAS you should ask the Department for Education and Skills (DfES) European Team for the form by telephoning 01325 391199, or it can be downloaded from the DfES site at **www.dfes.gov.uk/studentsupport/eustudents**.

If you have already started your course and are continuing, you should complete **form EU4(F)**, also available from the DfES or online.

You should return the appropriate form to the DfES together with any relevant documents as soon as possible, but no later than 31 May for courses that start in the autumn or 30 September for courses that start in the winter.

If you decide to change your course or withdraw from a course after having submitted your application form to the DfES European Team, you must notify them of this as soon as possible.

- **Contact:**
  DfES European Team
  2F-Area B, Mowden Hall, Staindrop Road, Darlington DL3 9BG

  (t) 01325 391199

  (e) euteam@dfes.gsi.gov.uk

  (↗) www.dfes.gov.uk/studentsupport/eustudents

  (The DfES's website contains specific information for each EU country.)

- **For details of financial support for study in Scotland, contact:**
  The Student Awards Agency for Scotland
  Gyleview House, 3 Redheughs Rigg, Edinburgh EH12 9HH

  (t) 0845 111 1711

  (e) saas.geu@scotland.gsi.gov.uk

  (↗) www.saas.gov.uk

- **For details of financial support for study in Northern Ireland, contact:**
  The Awards Section, Belfast Education and Library Board
  40 Academy Street, Belfast BT1 2NQ

  (t) 028 9056 4237

  (↗) www.student-support.org.uk

■ Part-time undergraduates

If you are an EU student on a part-time undergraduate course that is the equivalent of at least 50 per cent of a full-time course, you may apply to the discretionary **Access to Learning Fund** at your institution for a fee waiver if you are on an income of less than £14,200 per year.

Assistance from the fund is not guaranteed and students should speak to their students' union advice services for further guidance.

■ Student loans

Most EU students are not eligible for financial maintenance support from the student loan or Access to Learning Funds. Student loans are available to 'home students' only, i.e., those who are ordinarily resident in the UK on the first day of the first academic year of the course, and who have been resident in the UK during the three years immediately preceding their courses. They must also have **settled status** in the UK.

However, migrant workers from the European Economic Area (the EU countries, plus Norway, Switzerland and Lichtenstein) are exempted from the three years' ordinary residence period provided they came to the UK initially to work and not for education purposes, and who, after some time spent in employment, want to study on a vocational HE course related to their employment.

The time limit of a right to be classified as an EU migrant worker is up to six months from the date of arrival in the UK. Students should contact the LEA in whose area they live for an assessment form for eligibility for the student loan.

■ Postgraduate courses

Financial support for EU students does not extend to postgraduate study except for those on Postgraduate Certificates of Education (PGCE) courses. However, some of the Research Councils do provide funding to EU students for research. See **www.rcuk.ac.uk** for contact details.

If you cannot access financial support through the councils, contact the universities at which you wish to study about any scholarship schemes for EU students, or speak to the British Council, who can be contacted at **www.britishcouncil.org** or at the British Embassy in your country.

■ Initial Teacher Training

EU students attending full or part-time Initial Teacher Training Courses (ITT) in the UK (including PGCEs) are entitled to the full payment of their tuition fees (no means test applies). You should apply to the DfES's European Assessment Team (see above) for the appropriate form.

You are also entitled to apply for some of the financial incentives including the Secondary Shortage Subject Scheme (SSSS) offered to students undertaking ITT courses.

- **See pages 71–6 for more details or contact:**
  Teacher Training Agency
  - (t) 020 7925 3700 / 0845 6000 991
    Minicom: 01245 454 343
  - (↗) www.useyourheadteach.gov.uk

■ European Union Educational Mobility Programmes

The Commission of the EU finances schemes to promote educational and training programmes across Europe, including countries of Central and Eastern Europe.

For further information, including schemes for postgraduate funding, contact your own country's Ministry of Education or the British Council or The EU Cultural Action Unit, 120 Rue de Treves, B-1040 Brussels, Belgium.

- **In the UK, contact:**
  The British Council
  Bridgewater House, 58 Whitworth Street, Manchester M1 6BB
  - (t) 0161 957 7755
  - (f) 0161 957 7762
  - (e) general.enquiries@britishcouncil.org
  - (↗) www.britishcouncil.org/education **or** www.socrates-uk.net/

12 International students

It's all a little different for foreign students, and not necessarily in a good way either.

■ What's it going to cost?

If you are classified as an **international** or **overseas** student for fee purposes, you are not eligible for student support from the UK government and your fees are likely to be much higher than for home students.

In fact, you'll pay **full-cost tuition fees**, but because the universities set those fees individually, we can't give you precise figures. What we can give you is an indication of the tuition fee levels charged by public sector institutions for international students for the 2004/5 academic year; the more high-profile or private institutions may charge more:

Undergraduate:

- Classroom-based courses: £6,250–£8,000
- Laboratory-based courses: £6,500–£10,000
- Clinical Medical, Dental, Veterinary Science: £6,700–£18,500

Postgraduate:

- Classroom-based courses: £6,750–£8,400
- Laboratory-based courses: £6,500–£10,000
- Clinical courses in Medicine, Dentistry and Veterinary Science: £6,500–£17,500
- MBA courses: £7,500–£13,500

(Some high-profile business schools may charge up to £20,000 a year.)

Of course, you have to add to that your living costs and, according to estimates by the British Council, you should budget approximately

£6,650 in London and £5,250 elsewhere for a single student's average daily living costs during the academic year (nine months) in the UK.

■ Financial support from the UK government

It is possible for students born outside the UK and the EU to qualify for support from the UK government and for the lower 'home' fee rate.

The first step is that you must be **ordinarily resident** in the UK for the three years immediately before you start your course. Ordinary residence means lawful residence from choice for a settled purpose. You must also have **settled status**, effectively meaning that there is no time limit on your stay in the UK – your visa is not going to run out, for instance, or you have 'limited right to enter or remain' in the UK. If you have attended a course of full-time education during any part of the three-year period you will not qualify as ordinarily resident and will not be eligible for financial support or a reduced fee rate.

However, the rules are different for those who are officially recognised as refugees by the Home Office and European Economic Area (EEA, see above for the definition of that) or as migrant workers. Refugee students are eligible for the same assistance as home students from the moment they are recognised as refugees – that is, once you are granted Indefinite Leave to Remain status.

If you apply for asylum and are granted Humanitarian Protection or Discretionary Leave (or were previously granted Exceptional Leave to Remain or Enter), you have to meet, as with all other overseas students, the three-year residence requirement. However, you do not have to have settled status.

The only exception to this are those aged 16 or over and under 19 years of age and granted asylum who are studying an FE course in England. In this case you can apply to the college's Learner Support Fund for financial assistance, although there is no guarantee you will receive any money, since it's up to the college in question. Contact Student Services in the college for more information.

EEA migrant workers (those from the member states of the EU plus Norway, Iceland and Liechtenstein) are eligible for the full range of support, assuming you fulfil the residency requirement for EEA students (see pages 90 and 97 for that).

To check your Immigration Status contact the Immigration Status Enquiry Unit (ISEU) on 020 8760 8686.

As you'll have noticed, it's quite a tricky issue if you're an international student heading to these shores and the broad information in these pages cannot hope to cover every possible eventuality.

These organisations may be able to give more tailored advice:

- **Universities and Colleges Admissions Services (UCAS),**
  Rose Hill, New Barn Lane, Cheltenham, Gloucestershire GL52 3LZ

  (t) 0870 1122211

  (e) enquiries@ucas.ac.uk

  (↗) www.ucas.ac.uk

  For Further Education courses, contact the institution directly.

For more information on funding for international students, contact:

- **British Council**
  10 Spring Gardens, London, SW1A 2BN

  (t) (enquiries) 0161 957 7755

  (f) 0161 957 7762

  (↗) www.britishcouncil.org

  Funding database: ukscholarshipsdatabase.britishcouncil.org

For advice and information on sources of funding for refugees and asylum seekers, contact:

- **Refugee Education and Training Advisory Service (RETAS)**
  14 Dufferin Street, London EC1Y 8PD

  (t) Helpline: 020 7426 5801 (Tuesdays and Thursdays only, 2.30 p.m.–5 p.m.)

  (↗) www.education-action.org

For information about a wide variety of issues for overseas students, contact:

- **UKCOSA: The Council for International Education**
  9–17 St Alban's Place, London N1 0NX

  UKCOSA are able to offer advice on financial difficulties.

  (t) Helpline: 020 7107 9922 (1 p.m.–4 p.m. Monday to Friday)

  (↗) www.ukcosa.org.uk

■ Information on funding

The majority of scholarships for international students are for postgraduate courses. For information on awards/scholarships for attending undergraduate courses in the UK funded by international agencies such as UNESCO or the European Commission, you should contact your own country's Ministry of Education.

You might also get lucky with one of the following organisations:

Association of Commonwealth Universities

The ACU administers a wide range of scholarships and can provide information on universities throughout the Commonwealth. Full information on the exact details of the scholarships can be found at the website or by writing to the ACU. The main awards include:

- **Commonwealth Scholarship and Fellowship Plan for postgraduate study and research**. This was set up to enable highly promising students of Commonwealth countries to study at other Commonwealth countries' universities, including those in the UK. For information on courses and eligibility criteria for the UK contact the Commonwealth Scholarship Agency in your own country or visit **www.csfp-online.org/hostcountries/uk** for further details. A very small number of undergraduate awards are available through this scheme for students from some island nations and territories in the Atlantic and Indian Oceans

- **The British Marshall Scholarship** was set up in commemoration of the Marshall Aid programme's assistance to the UK after the Second World War. It is open to US citizens who have already achieved an undergraduate degree in the US and wish to pursue a postgraduate degree in the UK. About 40 scholarships are awarded each year. For further information contact the Commission's secretariat at the ACU address below or the relevant regional centre in the US (a list of these centres is available on the website).

(e) info@marshallscholarship.org (↗) www.marshallscholarship.org

The Association of Commonwealth Universities
36 Gordon Square, London WC1H OPF

(t) 020 7380 6700 (e) info@acu.ac.uk
(f) 020 7387 2655 (↗) www.acu.ac.uk

British Council scholarships and fellowships

The British Council offers full awards for courses of advanced study or research at universities or research institutions in Britain. These awards normally include fees, maintenance and travel, and are for one academic year in most cases.

Applications must be made to the British Council representative in your own country (or to the British Embassy if there is no British Council representative). Applications cannot be made from within the UK to the British Council Office.

The closing date for applications is usually the end of October of the year immediately preceding the start of the course, and it is advisable to begin making enquiries at least a year before the commencement of the course.

An address list of British Council offices around the globe can be accessed online at **www.britishcouncil.org**, or in writing from The British Council, Bridgewater House, 58 Whitworth Street, Manchester M1 6BB.

Like the ACU, the British Council also administers or provides information on a wide range of other scholarships. These include:

- **British Chevening Scholarships**. These are funded by the Foreign and Commonwealth Office and administered by the British Council. They are prestigious awards, which enable overseas students to study in the UK. Around 2,300 new scholarships are awarded each year for postgraduate studies or research at UK Institutions of Higher Education. For more information, contact:

The British Council
10 Spring Gardens, London SW1A 2BN

(t) (enquiries) 0161 957 7755   (e) general.enquiries@britishcouncil.org

(f) 0161 957 7762   (↗) www.chevening.com

- **The DfID Shared Scholarship Scheme** is funded jointly by the UK Department for International Development and participating UK universities to allow students from developing Commonwealth countries the chance to enrol on undergraduate and postgraduate courses in subjects relevant to the development of the student's country. Applicants must be under 35 and must speak fluent English. For further information on participating institutions, contact the British Council Office or British Embassy in your own country.

■ Other opportunities

Universities UK operate a fee-support scheme for overseas postgraduate research students. The awards cover the difference between home and overseas postgraduate tuition fees and are given on the basis of the candidate's academic merit and research potential. Applications must be made through the institution in the UK where you intend to study, on forms obtainable from that university's Registrar. Contact:

Universities UK
Woburn House, 20 Tavistock Square, London WC1H 9HQ

(t) 020 7419 4111   (e) ors_scheme@UniversitiesUK.ac.uk

(f) 020 7388 8649   (↗) www.universitiesuk.ac.uk/ors

The Soros Foundation
offers grants to students, especially those from Central and Eastern Europe and Central Asia, to enable them to study in other countries.

(↗) www.soros.org/grants

■ Exchange programmes

Students from Central/Eastern Europe should contact the British Council in their own country for information on the four exchange programmes: **Erasmus, Tempus, Lingua** and **Leonardo da Vinci**. These programmes were established in order to encourage mobility between the EU and the countries of Central and Eastern Europe. Applications have to be submitted by a student's institution (not by individual students). Further information on all these programmes is available from:

The British Council Education and Training Group
10 Spring Gardens, London SW1A 2BN

(t) (enquiries) 0161 957 7755   (e) general.enquiries@britishcouncil.org

(f) 0161 957 7762   (↗) www.britishcouncil.org

Information is also available from

The European Commission

(↗) www.europa.eu.int

■ Essential information

Before leaving for the UK, you must enquire at the British Embassy in your own country whether you are a **visa national** (that is, nationals of a country whose citizens must have a visa to enter the UK). If you are, you must obtain a visa; airlines and ships do not allow visa nationals to travel without a valid visa; nor would British port authorities allow you to enter.

If you do not require a visa to enter the UK (i.e., you are not a visa national) you should still try to obtain entry clearance from the British Embassy in your own country to make your arrival easier.

Remember to bring with you: your valid passport, letter or confirmation of enrolment on a full-time course, documentation of adequate financial resources and support during your stay in the UK (for example, a letter from your sponsor and/or confirmation of scholarship, and a bank statement).

From time to time, as a result of political developments, changes are made to the immigration rules; the British Embassy in your own country should be able to advise you on any recent changes.

■ Visa renewals

In July 2003 the Home Office announced that from 1 August 2003 it would charge foreign nationals for their applications for leave to remain in the UK (sometimes known as 'visa renewal'). The procedure was previously free of charge.

The charges will apply whether or not the application is successful. Applications made by post will cost £155, with what the Home Office call a 'premium' same-day service (going in person to one of the four processing centres in Croydon, Birmingham, Glasgow or Liverpool) costing £250. Appeals against visa decisions will not carry any charges.

For postal applications the Home Office guarantee a response within 13 weeks, with a target of 70 per cent being processed within three weeks. Payment can be made by cheque, banker's draft, postal order or by debit or credit card. Cash and banker's drafts from foreign banks are not acceptable forms of payment, and the case will not be considered until the payment has cleared – so effectively you cannot pay by cheque on 'premium' applications.

There are some groups who will be exempt from charges for postal applications (but not for the 'premium' service): those applying for asylum; nationals of Bulgaria and Turkey and their dependants applying for leave to remain; and those applying for indefinite leave to remain on the grounds of domestic violence and where they appear to be destitute.

13 Postgraduates

It would be forgivable – even normal – to assume that a good degree, a genuine interest in your subject and a carefully thought-out research plan would pretty much guarantee postgraduate funding. But, especially now and especially for arts subjects, this is very far from the case.

For many subjects the only central source of funding is the massively oversubscribed **Arts and Humanities Research Board (AHRB)**, which awards fees and maintenance grants to UK residents. Around a quarter of applicants for Competition A (masters level) funding are successful. Things are slightly easier for scientists, with a wider range of research boards to aim for and with a greater chance of industry funding.

To be in with even a reasonable chance of securing funding requires an excellent academic record, superb references and an enthusiastic reception from the institution where you will be studying. To strengthen the application, make sure – and make sure the board knows – that the research plan fits exactly with the expertise of the department. This applies across all subjects

References must also be extremely detailed – a one-line scrawl proclaiming that this is a first-class student will no longer suffice. They have to explain exactly why a candidate is not only academically qualified, but also suited to exactly this project.

There are seven main award-making bodies. Applications are either made through the college department where you intend to study or to the awarding body, rather than direct to the award-making body. To qualify for a studentship you will need at least an upper second-class honours degree, and more usually a first. As we said, competition for awards is now very intense.

The main research boards are:

- **Arts and Humanities Research Board**
  Whitefriars, Lewins Mead,
  Bristol BS1 2AE

  (t) 0117 987 6543

  (f) 0117 987 6544

  (↗) www.ahrb.ac.uk

- **The Natural Environment Research Council**
  Polaris House, North Star Avenue,
  Swindon SN2 1EU

  (t) 01793 411500

  (f) 01793 411501

  (↗) www.nerc.ac.uk

- **Medical Research Council**
  20 Park Crescent,
  London W1B 1AL

  (t) 020 7636 5422

  (f) 020 7436 6179

  (↗) www.mrc.ac.uk

- **Particle Physics and Astronomy Research Council**
  Polaris House, North Star Avenue,
  Swindon SN2 1SZ

  (t) 01793 442000

  (f) 01793 442125

  (↗) www.pparc.ac.uk

- **Engineering and Physical Sciences Research Council**
  Polaris House, North Star Avenue,
  Swindon SN2 1ET

  (t) 01793 444000
     Helpline: 01793 444100

  (e) studentships@epsrc.ac.uk

  (↗) www.epsrc.ac.uk

- **Biotechnology and Biological Sciences Research Council**
  Polaris House, North Star Avenue,
  Swindon SN2 1UH

  (t) 01793 413200

  (f) 01793 413201

  (↗) www.bbsrc.ac.uk

- **Economic and Social Research Council**
  Polaris House, North Star Avenue,
  Swindon SN2 1UJ

  (t) 01793 413000

  (f) 01793 413001

  (↗) www.esrc.ac.uk

Interdisciplinary studentships are offered by some funders; for example, ESRC/NERC. Ask funders for details.

These councils fund Research Studentships, which cover fees and maintenance and Masters Studentships covering taught course fees and maintenance. The levels of funding (2004/5 rate) are:

		Research Studentships £	Masters Studentships £
AHRB	(London)	12,500	10,100
	(outside London)	10,500	8,100
ESRC	(London)	11,000	
	(outside London)	9,000	
NERC	(London)	14,500	9,500
	(outside London)	12,500	7,500
MRC	(London)	12,500	12,500
	(outside London)	10,500	10,500
EPSRC	Engineering Doctorates only	10,500	12,000
PPARC	(London)	12,500	
	(outside London)	10,500	
BBSRC	(London)	12,500	12,500
	(outside London)	10,500	10,500
	Students with veterinary degrees only (all of UK)	17,020	17,020

Note that the EPSRC and MRC have changed funding so that individual institutions will be allocated block grants from which they then set the number of studentships and the level of stipend. A minimum level of stipend is set as indicated above, with institutions deciding whether to grant more than this depending on local circumstances. The EPSRC set no minimum payment for Masters Studentships.

The BBSRC has a similar scheme to the MRC and EPSRC in respect of its doctoral (research) studentships only. The minimum level of bursary is set as indicated in the table.

■ Postgraduate bursaries

The **General Social Care Council** (**GSCC**) awards bursaries to full-time postgraduate students studying on approved social work courses. All students receive a basic grant for living costs, which for 2004/5 is £2,900 if you live away from home in London; £2,500 if you live away from home outside London; and £2,100 if you live with your parents. You are also given a travel allowance for placement work and your tuition fees are paid in full (paid straight to your university).

There is a supplementary means-tested award for poorer students and several other allowances for students with dependants, older students and students with disabilities. Contact:

GSCC Bursaries Office
Goldings House, 2 Hay's Lane, London SE1 2HBE

(t) Bursary Information Line: 020 7397 5835
(10 a.m.–12 p.m., 2 p.m.–4 p.m.)

(e) bursaries@gscc.org.uk

(↗) www.gscc.org.uk/bursaries.htm

■ Other options

The next port of call is **internal funding**, with scholarships offered by many universities for both UK and overseas students, sometimes fees-only, sometimes also for living costs.

But be warned: universities being as vulnerable as anyone else to plunging stock markets, some have less to hand out than usual. There are usually three types of studentships that universities can hand out:

- **Three-year studentships**, i.e., for the duration of a course. This is awarded to a new student

- **One-year studentships** – for those students who wish to do extra research (or more often for those who have not completed their research in three years and who have run out of funding). Sometimes one-year studentships may be awarded for one year taught courses

- **Postgraduate Teaching and Research Assistantships** – where postgraduate students are employed by the institution to undertake specific teaching or research duties in return for a reduced salary and/or waiving of tuition fees, etc.

Contact the department to enquire about any schemes which may be available.

Funds are sometimes available from trusts and charities, but these rarely cover the full cost of fees and maintenance. You might find the following useful if looking for charitable funding:

- **The Educational Grants Directory**
  Published annually by the
  Directory of Social Change (DSC).

  (t) 08450 77 77 07

  (↗) www.dsc.org.uk

- **A Guide to Grants for Individuals in Need**
  Published annually by the DSC
  (see above)

- **Directory of Grant-Making Trusts**
  Published annually by the DSC
  (see above)

- **Charities Digest**
  Published by Waterlow's
  Legal Publishing

  (t) 020 7549 8670

  (↗) www.waterlow.com

- **The Grants Register**
  Published annually by Palgrave
  Macmillan Publishers Ltd.
  This is particularly relevant to
  postgraduate student awards
  tenable in the UK and overseas.
  Available at any large public library.

  (↗) www.palgrave.com

- **Study Abroad**
  Published by the United Nations
  Educational Scientific and Cultural
  Organisation (UNESCO)

  (↗) www.upo.unesco.org

- **International Awards 2001**
  Published by the Association of
  Commonwealth Universities (ACU)
  and available in most university
  libraries or British Council Offices.

  (↗) www.acu.ac.uk/yearbook
  /awards.html

- **Scholarships for Study in the USA and Canada**
  Published by Peterson's: includes
  details of scholarships and financial
  aid for international students
  (including those from the UK)
  wishing to study in North America.

  (↗) www.petersons.com

- **British and International Music Yearbook** and **British Music Education Yearbook**
  Both published by Rhinegold

  (↗) www.rhinegold.co.uk

For more advice on alternative sources of funding, please contact:

The Educational Grants Advisory Service (EGAS)
501–505 Kingsland Road, London E8 4AU

(t) Helpline: 020 7254 6251
   (10 a.m.–12 p.m., 2 p.m.–4 p.m. Mondays, Wednesdays and Fridays)

(↗) www.egas-online.org

Useful websites for charities and educational grants include:

- **www.funderfinder.org.uk**
- **www.scholarship-search.org.uk**

Failing that, for those undiscouraged by years of undergraduate debt, there are **career development loans** (see page 86 for details). You are not eligible for student loans unless you are undertaking a course of initial teacher training. In general, full-time postgraduate students are not able to access state benefits. However, there are some exceptions to this rule, such as lone parents and students with certain disabilities (see page 160–62 for details).

■ Self-funding

There remains the possibility of going it alone, at least to start with – the separate categories for doctoral and masters-level funding mean it is possible to apply again for Ph.D. funding if you are unsuccessful the first time around.

The worst-case scenario leaves you with the burden of both fees – usually around £3,000 a year for an M.Phil./Ph.D. for UK citizens – plus living costs.

University College London estimates you need £8,760 a year to live in London; it would be rather less outside the capital. Many students rely on loans or gifts from family, savings or bank overdrafts. Others work, either in conjunction with a part-time masters or Ph.D., or in what free time can be eked from a full-time course. To make life harder, even for students, anything earned over the personal allowance of £4,615 incurs income tax (and National Insurance).

There are some opportunities within the universities. Some university departments offer full **demonstratorships** (similar to teaching and research assistantships, see above), covering tuition fees and a stipend in return for a certain number of hours a year of teaching or demonstrating. Teaching assistantships normally involve teaching undergraduates, marking coursework and grading exams, but are often only available to those who have completed at least a year of the M.Phil./Ph.D. programme.

Then there are the external options. Specialised work will obviously pay better than the stereotypical student options – bartender, shop assistant, etc. – and so require much less time out of the course. Some companies provide scholarships on day-release schemes or on the understanding that you will join the company on graduating and possibly carry out your research on a subject of interest to them.

■ Access to Learning Funds (ALF)

Access to Learning Funds are discretionary funds administered by institutions designed to help students in financial difficulty or who have unexpected costs they cannot cover from their own student support. Part-time and full-time postgraduates are eligible to apply for these funds, but they will expect you to have made 'reasonable provision' for your own tuition fees and living costs as the ALF is not intended to fully support postgraduate study (see pages 87–91 for more details).

■ Disabled Students' Allowance

Full and part-time postgraduate students who are studying 'recognised' taught and research courses are eligible for a Disabled Students' Allowance. The course should be eligible for awards from the research councils or equivalent to a course that is eligible for awards. It should be at least one academic year in length if full-time. Part-time courses should be for longer than a year, but not more than twice as long as an equivalent full-time course. Existing and new students are eligible and there is no age limit. See pages 25–6 for details.

■ Postgraduate studies in Scotland

The SAAS supports some postgraduate study in Scotland. For specific advice regarding such study, you should contact the SAAS direct on 0845 111 1711. Bursaries for social work courses are also provided by the Scottish Social Services Council (see page 114).

Vocational diplomas

Awards for study in a range of vocational postgraduate courses in Scotland, mainly at diploma level, is funded by the SAAS. This is called the Postgraduate Student Allowances Scheme (PSAS). Awards are limited and competition for them is high.

The SAAS also fund a small number of such places in institutions elsewhere in the UK. Contact the SAAS for more details; a guidance booklet can be downloaded from their website (**www.student-support -saas.gov.uk**).

Postgraduate Certificates of Education

Scottish students starting a Postgraduate Certificate of Education (PGCE) in Scotland directly after completing an undergraduate degree course will continue to be supported on the same basis. You should contact the SAAS for precise guidance, especially if you wish to begin a PGCE course some time after having completing an undergraduate degree.

Scottish studentships

If you wish to secure funding for either a doctorate or research studentship you should contact the department you wish to study within or the research board or council appropriate to the subject, for information on the awards available. The SAAS no longer funds studentships directly.

Social work bursaries in Scotland

The Scottish Social Services Council (SSSC) will pay the tuition fees of all Scottish students on recognised postgraduate social work courses in Scotland. In addition, they also award means-tested maintenance awards of up to £3,480 for 30 weeks' study (with additional allowances for longer courses). The amount received will be dependent on whether you live with your parents or not, your income and that of your parents or spouse where applicable. There are supplementary allowances if you are an older student, if you have any dependants, if you have any disabilities and if you have extra travel costs. For more information, contact:

The Scottish Social Services Council
Compass House, 11 Riverside Drive, Dundee DD1 4NY

(t) 0845 60 30 891   (e) enquiries@sssc.uk.com   (↗) www.sssc.uk.com

■ Postgraduate studies in Northern Ireland

Apart from initial teacher training, the student support system for postgraduate students in Northern Ireland is limited to studentships and research grants administered by DELNI, the Research Councils, the Arts and Humanities Research Board and some other charitable sources.

However, Disabled Students' Allowances (DSAs) are available if you are a postgraduate student.

14 Further education students

England

■ Support for 16–19-year-olds only

Fees

If you are under 19 on the 31 August before your enrolment, beginning either a full or part-time FE course funded by the Learning and Skills Council (LSC), you do not have to pay tuition fees. Some private colleges may ask for a fee.

Schools' access funds

LEAs administer a needs-based fund for pupils aged 16–19 in schools. The funds are aimed at targeting groups with low staying-on rates, but high achievers should not be excluded. Criteria are at the discretion of the LEAs and payments are in the form of grants. Check with your LEAs for eligibility criteria.

Education Maintenance Allowances (EMA)

The EMA is a statutory financial award that aims to support young people from low-income households who undertake full-time courses in Further Education. It consists of:

- a weekly payment of up to £30 (during term time only)
- intermittent bonuses of £100.

The EMA is paid for two years, although a third year may be possible depending on your circumstances.

In order to apply for the EMA you must meet the course and personal eligibility criteria:

Course requirements

You must be participating in a programme of full-time education at a recognised school, sixth form college or FE college. You cannot be in receipt of any DfES funding or other government funding which would not allow you to additionally receive an EMA, such as a Dance and Drama Award or Jobseeker's Allowance.

Residence requirements

You must be either a UK citizen or a citizen of the European Economic Area (the countries of the European Union plus Norway, Iceland and Liechtenstein) and in either case have been resident in the UK or EEA for the last three years, or an officially recognised refugee, or have been granted Indefinite Leave to Remain or Temporary Protection (if you have to ask, you probably don't qualify).

Age requirements

In the areas where the scheme *was not* previously piloted, you are eligible for an EMA if you turn 17 between 1 September 2004 and 31 August 2005.

In the 56 local education authority areas where the scheme was piloted in the 2003/4 academic year, it is available if you turn 17, 18 or 19 during that time, or if you turn 20 and have a letter from a Connexions personal adviser stating you should be eligible. Details of which areas were in the pilot are available on the EMA website at **www.ema.dfes.gov.uk**.

Payments

Payments are available for up to two years (or possibly longer at the discretion of your LEA) and are dependent on your fulfilling the conditions laid out in your EMA contract (see below). How much you receive depends on your household income, which is assessed at the start of the year.

The income assessed is that of your parents, guardians or other main carers. **If you live with only one parent**, your other parent will not be assessed and any maintenance they pay will not be counted as income.

The calculation is based on the income made in the preceding full tax year, so for applications for autumn 2004 this would be the tax year 2003/4. Any income you have (from a part-time job, for example) is not included.

If you live with foster parents or are in the care of the local authority, you will automatically receive the full EMA, although you will have to provide proof of your status, such as a letter from the local authority.

If you do not live with your parents or other carers and receive income support, you will automatically receive the full EMA.

If you are a parent and you care for the child yourself, you will be assessed on your own income in the same way as your parents would.

If your household has applied for tax credits, all you will need to submit is the Tax Credit Award Notice, otherwise you, your parents or carers will need to send appropriate evidence such as a **P60 form**. Social Security benefits, including Child Benefit, are disregarded in calculating your household income. The EMA payments are disregarded for the purpose of calculating your family's entitlement to means-tested benefits. Therefore if you or your family are claiming benefits you will be able to receive an EMA in addition to them.

The full EMA payment of £30 a week is available if you have a gross (before tax) household income of £19,630 a year or less.

A payment of £20 a week is made if you have a gross household income of between £19,631 and £24,030.

A payment of £10 a week is made if you have a gross household income of between £24,031 and £30,000.

If you have a gross household income of over £30,000 a year, you will not be eligible for the EMA.

All payments are made directly into your bank account, so you may need to open one.

In January and July of each year a £100 bonus is available if you have met the goals set out by the school or college in your EMA contract (see below). A further £100 bonus is available in September if you are returning for a second or third year of study to encourage you to return after the summer break.

EMA contract

In order to receive your weekly EMA payments and the bonuses, you must sign an EMA contract. These are provided by your school or college and set out what you are expected to achieve in terms of attendance and academic work.

This document is signed by you, your parents (or another responsible adult) and the education provider. No EMA is payable unless a contract is signed.

If you fail to meet part of the contract in any week (for example, fail to attend classes or hand in homework), you will not be paid your EMA for that week and it may be taken into account when deciding if you should receive your next bonus.

Applications

To apply for the scheme, contact your school, college or LEA and request a pack. Further details can also be found at the DfES website: **www.ema.dfes.gov.uk**.

Care to Learn

Care to Learn is a scheme introduced by the DfES to help young parents pay for childcare costs while in full or part-time education. The scheme will pay for the costs of registered childcare while you are at school, college or on placement. This will include fees that must be paid during holidays, and the cost of transport to and from the childcare provider, up to a maximum of £5,125 per child. It will not affect or be affected by Social Security Benefits.

You can apply if you are aged under 19 on 1 August 2004, living in England and caring for your own children. You must wish to start or continue a publicly funded course at school, sixth form college or an FE college. The scheme will only fund registered or approved childcare. If you have an informal childcare arrangement you may still apply for support through the Learner Support Funds.

Further information (including application information) can be accessed at **www.dfes.gov.uk/caretolearn** or by phoning the helpline on 0845 600 2809.

Transport

LEAs continue to have responsibility for ensuring adequate provision of home to school or college transport for those aged 16 to 19, although this might not be free. Contact your college or LEA for further information or go to **www.dfes.gov.uk/16-19transport** for details of local policies.

Asylum seekers

Although most public funds are not available to asylum seekers, if you are an asylum seeker aged 16 or over and under 19, you can apply to college Learner Support Funds.

■ Support for those aged 19+ only

Tuition fees

Colleges can opt into a voluntary system of fee remission for those aged 19+ who are:

- ☑ on means-tested benefits and Jobseeker's Allowance
- ☑ unwaged dependants of those on benefits and JSA
- ☑ taking programmes where the primary learning objective is adult basic education
- ☑ undertaking English courses because they not currently fluent in that language.

If colleges opt in to this system and you fall into one of the above categories, you are exempt from fee payment and the LSC will compensate the college for the cost of your fees. Contact colleges for details of provision.

If you are not in any of the above groups you may have to pay tuition fees. If you are having problems meeting the costs of fees, approach your college's student services to enquire about help, for example through the Learner Support Funds .

■ Support for all FE students

College Learner Support Funds

Learner Support Funds (LSFs) are monies given to colleges by the LSC to distribute to students in need. They are given in three pools:

- Hardship funds
- Residential bursaries
- Childcare bursaries.

Hardship funds

Hardship funds are open to all students studying at a college who meet the personal, residential and course conditions (see page 11, and 87–91 for details). It is down to the discretion of the college as to how their money will be spent from their hardship fund and you need to apply to your college. The upshot of this is that we can't tell you exactly what is available, but colleges tend to spend money in areas such as:

- means-tested bursaries to students
- purchasing 'benefits' or support for students – they may subsidise cheap transport or offer equipment at low cost
- childcare costs.

If you are a recipient of an Education Maintenance Allowance, you may receive grant payments from the Learner Support Funds if you can demonstrate that you have extra costs not provided for by your EMA payment. In exceptional cases, a loan may be provided from the funds. Contact your college's student services for details.

Residential bursaries

Some colleges offering courses in areas such as agriculture, art and design or other specialist subjects and which may require you to live and study away from home may offer bursaries for full-time study and may also be given for travel costs if you have to live at home but travel significant distances to college.

Childcare bursaries

Childcare bursaries of up to £4,000 per child can be used to meet the costs of any registered childcare. Funds can be paid directly to the childcare provider or given to you to pay them (but pay them you must!). Contact college student services for more details.

Informal childcare may be paid for from the funds if registered childcare is not available and the college authorises the arrangement. If you are under 19 you should apply to the Care to Learn scheme (see page 120) for registered care.

Dance and drama awards

Specific awards are available if you wish to study on courses leading to qualifications in dance, drama and stage management. Funding is available through selected, approved schools for between one and three years of study, for those who are aged 16 and over for dance courses or 18 and over for drama-related courses. There are a limited number of awards granted each year, and they are generally issued to those who show exceptional talent in an audition. All very Billy Elliott.

More information on these is available through the participating dance and drama schools or by visiting the DfES website at **www.dfes.gov.uk/dancedrama** (where you'll also find a list of the schools).

■ State benefits and tax credits

Full-time study

Most full-time students are ineligible to receive most Social Security Benefits. However, there are significant exceptions to this rule, especially if you have certain disabilities or dependent children. Check with the College Student Services or your local Job Centre Plus. If you have children you may be eligible for Child Tax Credits while studying full-time. See pages 157–60 for details.

New Deal

It may be possible to study under the New Deal schemes for 18–24s and 25+. Both schemes have a **Full-Time Education** and **Training Option** that enables you to study for up to a year to enhance your employability. Entry to either scheme depends on the period for which you have been in receipt of Jobseeker's Allowance – or in the case of the 25+ scheme, any equivalent such as Income Support. For the 18–24 scheme, you will usually need to have been unemployed for six months. For the 25+ scheme you should have received JSA or an equivalent for 18 months of the previous 21.

For both schemes the New Deal Adviser on the 'Gateway' will have discretion to consider approving a higher-level qualification if you already have the usual 'maximum' target skill level for the scheme (NVQ Level 2 – GCSE grades A–C or equivalent – for the 18–24 scheme and NVQ Level 3 – A-Level or equivalent – for the 25+ scheme). Contact your local Job Centre Plus for further details or visit the New Deal website at **www.newdeal.gov.uk**.

Part-time study

It may be possible to study part-time while claiming Jobseeker's Allowance or Income Support. But (and it may be a big but), it is not an *entitlement* under JSA regulations – the Job Centre Plus will need to be satisfied that your course is in fact part-time (see pages 160–64 for the definitions of full-time and part-time as far as benefits go). In addition, you will still need to be available for and actively seeking work. Contact your student union or college student services for advice on this issue.

National traineeships and modern apprenticeships

Both schemes are for 16–24 year olds to learn job-related skills and gain work experience. More information is available from the DfES website: **www.dfes.gov.uk/youngpeople/**.

Discretionary awards

Colleges may have other discretionary funds for students. For details, please enquire at college student services.

■ Alternative Sources

Career Development Loans (CDLs)

The Department for Education and Skills (DfES), in participation with three major banks (Barclays, The Co-operative and the Royal Bank of Scotland) operates a deferred repayment loan system. Between £300 and £8,000 can be borrowed towards fees and other expenses for students on full-time, part-time and vocational distance learning courses lasting up to two years (and up to one year's practical work experience where it is part of the course).

Degree and postgraduate courses are included. Throughout the period of study and up to one month after completing or leaving the course, the DfES pays your interest. Repayments are fixed and can be spread between one and five years. If you are registered unemployed at the end of the first month of completing your course, you may apply to the bank for deferment of repayment for up to five months initially, and for two further extensions of six months each.

Note that, unlike undergraduate student loans, applicants for a CDL are credit scored and they may be reluctant to offer a loan if you have a poor credit history, although you are advised to discuss any such history with one of the banks beforehand as refusal is not guaranteed. For further information call 0800 585 505 or visit the CDL website at **www.lifelonglearning.co.uk/cdl/**.

Professional studies loan schemes

Four of the major high street banks (HSBC, Barclays, NatWest and Lloyds TSB) offer professional studies loans. Some schemes are specifically aimed at study within certain fields (for example, Medicine, Dentistry, Law, Veterinary Science and Architecture), but some banks now offer loans for general vocational study. Loans up to £20,000 are available; interest rates and repayment terms are variable. Contact a local branch or visit the website of any of the above banks for more information.

Educational charities

Educational charities may offer small sums of money to contribute towards study costs. Demand for funds is high, so it is advisable to apply early. Most larger public libraries will hold one or more of the following publications:

A Guide to Grants for Individuals in Need Published annually by the Directory of Social Change

The Educational Grants Directory Published annually by the Directory of Social Change

The Grants Register Published by Macmillan Publishers Ltd

Directory of Grant Making Trusts Published by the Charities Aid Foundation

Charities Digest Published by Waterlow Information Services

Institutions, student unions, careers services or Citizens Advice Bureaux may have funding databases that match funding sources with specific needs. See page 83–6 for more details of alternative sources of funding.

 Contact

■ **LearnDirect**

  (t) 0800 100 900

  (↗) www.learndirect.co.uk

■ **Department for Education and Skills (DfES)**

  (t) 0870 000 2288
  Textphone: 01928 794 274
  Minicom: 0845 6055560

  (e) info@dfes.gsi.gov.uk

  (↗) www.dfes.gov.uk

■ **Learning and Skills Council**

  (t) 0870 900 6800

  (e) info@lsc.gov.uk

  (↗) www.lsc.gov.uk

■ **Education Maintenance Allowances**

  (t) 0808 101 6219

  (↗) www.ema.dfes.gov.uk

■ **Care to Learn**

  (t) 0845 600 2809

  (↗) www.dfes.gov.uk/caretolearn

■ **New Deal**

  (↗) www.newdeal.gov.uk

  Booklets (contact LearnDirect or the DfES for copies):

  Financial Help for Students (16–19)

  Money to Learn: Financial Help for Adults in Further Education and Training

Wales

Welsh students have separate but broadly similar schemes to those in England to fund them in further education. Contact your college or local education authority for more information.

Students on a low income may also be able to apply for an **Assembly Learning Grant** (see page 26).

Scotland

Tuition fees

The Scottish Further Education Funding Council (SFEFC) will pay the tuition fees for students on all full-time further education courses, regardless of age or previous courses of study. SFEFC will also pay the tuition fees of asylum seekers on part-time courses. Other students on part-time courses may be eligible for a fee waiver if they can demonstrate to their college that their income and personal circumstances would merit this. The college will then apply to SFEFC for the funding on the student's behalf.

Education Maintenance Allowances

EMAs in Scotland run on the same general principles as in England but there are some differences (particularly in terms of eligibility). Go to **www.emascotland.com** to find out more.

Maintenance bursaries

A full-time FE student in Scotland may apply for a means-tested bursary to support living costs. Colleges administer the bursaries and applications should be directed to the bursary officer in the college to which a course application has been made – except if you wish to study in Orkney or Shetland, where bursaries are administered by the local authority.

The colleges have considerable discretion over bursary awards, though they cannot award more than you are eligible for under the funding council's policy. If you are eligible for an **Education Maintenance Allowance** (**EMA**), you should apply for this in the first instance (see pages 117–20). Students in receipt of an EMA are not eligible for the maintenance bursaries (see below), although you may be eligible for supplementary help, for example, if you live away from your parents' home, or for extra travel and study costs.

Awards are issued to three different categories of students:

Category A: Students under 18 years of age who are parentally dependent and ineligible for an EMA

Category B: Students aged 18 or over who are parentally dependent

Category C: Independent students under 26 years of age and all students aged 26 or over.

The amount you receive depends on your status and household income. If you fall into category A or B you are assessed for support using your parents' income, and you will be assumed to live in the parental home and receive the lower rate (see below).

However, if you live out with a reasonable travelling distance to the college you will be able to receive the higher rate. If you fall into category C you will be assessed on your own income and that of your spouse or partner where applicable, and you will receive only the higher rate.

If you are under 26 you are regarded as 'independent' if you have supported yourself from your own income for three years or longer; are married or living with a partner as married; or both your parents are either no longer living or permanently estranged from you.

Support will normally be granted for one course of study only, and for courses that lead to qualification up to, but not including, Higher National Certificate level or towards a vocational qualification. If there has been a previous award, some colleges will consider a new application, providing a period of seven years has elapsed since the last award.

Bursaries are normally only awarded if your course is validated or examined by the Scottish Qualifications Authority (SQA). Where SQA provision is not available, awards may be given by other appropriate examining associations.

Colleges may withhold payments if you do not maintain satisfactory levels of conduct, attendance or progress without sufficient explanation. To avoid this happening, you should inform the college as soon as possible of any circumstances that might affect payment.

If you stay in a college residence, the college has the discretion to award you an allowance which corresponds to the rent for the residence plus a weekly personal allowance of £17.27, which would be paid instead of the rates set out below.

Colleges can only award a bursary to you if you fulfil the residential requirements. You will need to fulfil one of the following requirements:

- ✓ be ordinarily resident in Scotland on the qualifying date and to have been ordinarily resident in the British Isles throughout the period of three years preceding that date

- ✓ be entitled to equality of treatment by virtue of EU regulations and ordinarily resident in the European Economic Area (EEA) or Switzerland throughout the period immediately preceding the relevant date

- ✓ be a refugee, who has been ordinarily resident in the British Isles at all times since you were first recognised as a refugee, or the spouse or child of such a refugee.

The rates are:

Category	Standard (at home) rate	Higher (away from home) rate
A	£25.00	£56.31
B	£62.32	£78.77
C	N/A	£78.77

The figures are the maximum rates per week, although bursary money is usually paid to you on a monthly basis. The amount you receive will depend on your household income.

If you are an EMA student living away from your parents' home because your college is not within reasonable travelling distance, you may be eligible for an away-from-home allowance of up to £31.31 a week, in addition to your EMA.

Dependants' allowances

If you have a dependent spouse or other adult, you may be able to claim an allowance of up to £44.90 a week. You cannot claim dependants' allowances for more than one adult or for anyone who already gets student support.

If you have dependent children, you should claim for extra help through the tax credits system.

Other allowances

Colleges have the discretion to award further allowances in respect of travel, study expenses and special educational need. The amount you receive will vary depending on your circumstances and need.

Part-time students

If you are a part-time FE student you may be able to claim some allowances for travel, study costs and for extra costs if you have a disability or special educational need. Ask your college for details.

Childcare fund

You can apply to the college for assistance with childcare costs incurred as a result of your attendance at college. Award policy in individual colleges can vary and they might apply additional residential or other criteria. Consult the students' association or college in the first instance.

Hardship funds

Scottish institutions of further and higher education receive money from the Scottish Executive to provide extra help for all home students who experience financial hardship. You can be on a full- or part-time course, but you must be at least 16 years of age.

FE colleges may also award hardship funds to you if you are an asylum seeker and on a full- or part-time English as a Second or Other Language (ESOL) course or any other part-time course of non-advanced education. Other foreign nationals on ESOL courses may also apply, provided their main purpose of residence in the UK is not education. Demand varies from institution to institution and each will have its own criteria for distribution of funds. Contact the students' association or the institution itself for further information.

Charities and trusts

Various charities and trusts have been set up to assist both Scottish students and those who study in Scotland. You should consult your local public or institution library for copies of *The Educational Grants Directory*, published annually by the Directory of Social Change (call 08450 77 77 07 or visit **www.dsc.org.uk**). See pages 83–6 for more details on alternative sources of funding.

Career Development Loans   See page 88.

Professional studies loan schemes   See pages 88 and 125.

Northern Ireland

Tuition fees

Tuition fees have been formally abolished for full-time students aged over 19 on eligible vocational FE courses at level 3 and below. However, this does not include academic courses such as GCSE, A-level or level 4 or above.

If you are still required to pay a fee and are on a low income, you may be able to receive assistance from your college's support funds. See below for further details.

Education Maintenance Allowances

As with Scotland the EMAs in NI are different but similar to those in England. Go to **www.emani.gov.uk** for full details.

Discretionary bursaries

If you do not qualify for an EMA, you may be able to receive a discretionary bursary. There are two types of bursary, both administered by ELBs:

Full Value awards

These bursaries are available if you are studying on an eligible advanced course. They are means-tested, and the maximum bursary in the 2004/5 academic year is £1,056 if you live at your parent's home and £1,332 if you do not. Speak to your college to see if your course is eligible.

Further Education bursaries

These bursaries are awarded on the same basis as Higher Education bursaries (see page 58 for details).

You should apply early for both bursaries as funds are limited and may run out. Extra allowances are available if you have extra costs associated with a disability or you have recently left care.

Learner support funds See page 91 for details.

Part 2
Keep it

Holding on to your cash
and spending it wisely

1 Money

■ Gap years

A quick word before you go...

In almost any year other than 2005, the advice to students considering a gap year would be simple – go for it! This time round, it's all a little different.

As you should know by now, from 2006 students taking up a place will be liable for tuition fees of up to £3,000 a year. So taking a gap year now for deferred entry in 2006 could drop you into some major debt later. You have to balance that thought with the tantalising possibilities that taking up to 15 months off wherever you like can offer.

If you do decide to take a gap 'year' longer than nine months before you start your course, you should make sure you have as much proof as possible of your intended return to the UK for study. This might include evidence of having secured deferred entry to your chosen institution and/or tickets with a specific date of return. In the past, some LEAs have not accepted that a period abroad of longer than 9 months is a temporary absence and have therefore disqualified some students from tuition fee support and student loans on the grounds that they do not fulfil the residency requirement for such support. This can be challenged, but the more proof you can supply that the absence was temporary, the more likely the success of any such challenge. Contact your local NUS Welfare Unit for more details if you think this might be a problem for you.

As likely as not, you'll need to address the question before sending in your UCAS application (so we may be too late – well meaning, but useless). At the applications stage, careers advisers may ask what you plan to gain from the time off. Let's not pretend jetting around the world will make you a better person: it won't. Whether admissions tutors genuinely think that travel broadens the mind is debatable; perhaps they simply hope that next year's freshers will get the worst excesses of drug-taking and sexual abandon out of the way on some foreign beach rather than on campus. Either way, such concerns shouldn't cloud your horizon.

Put simply, there are few times in your life when you can doss around abroad and maintain a socially acceptable CV. Career breaks may be possible in theory; in practice, the numbers who get round to taking six months to go travelling later in life are comparatively few. While money may well be tight now and there's the prospect of mounting student debt to come, most school-leavers will have fewer ties now than in the family/mortgage/career-burdened future. And having a place secured at university pre-empts the worst angst of all travellers: what to do when you get home.

Once you've decided to take the plunge, you must first solve the big killer question: how to fund your trip. The classic route is to take advantage of a rent-free parental environment and get your head down for a long slog of paid work. But if staying a few more months at home seems a heavy price to pay for the time ahead, you should be encouraged by the deals and financial cushions open to students and those under 26.

Raising money and making the cash go further might prove easier under the aegis of charitable organisations. Raleigh International and Project Trust are perhaps the best known of the many organisations looking for volunteers to work overseas on conservation or charity projects. Typically, you raise an initial sum and then work for three months with all accommodation and subsistence provided, but your travel tickets will allow you to stay abroad and do your own thing for much longer. The structure and support the charities offer, and the environmental and community projects they run, mean you're likely to get something more tangible than a suntan from your trip. And raising sponsorship could be both quicker and more enjoyable than saving for months in a menial job.

If you don't want to commit to a long-term project abroad, travelling and working as you go is a possibility. Making your way to Australia for a working stop on a round-the-world trip is the classic option, attractive not least for sunshine in January – and again, it's easier when you're young as the temporary work visas are only normally issued to people under 30. You'll also find the exchange rate is still pretty favourable to Brits heading that way. Either way, you need £2,000 and an onward airline ticket to get a visa for Australia.

Remember, too, that working abroad can sound a lot more glamorous than it is. Sorting out the bureaucracy through an organisation like BUNAC might help you get established in a job in the United States, but there are a lot of unhappy au pairs out there. And holiday firms offering courier or chalet jobs are likely to pay you an absolute pittance, although they can be a lot of fun. Try to speak to your predecessors or current incumbents in any such job to work out just what the costs and rewards might be. Resorts have their own economy, and things like customer tips or free beer at a bar can make or break you on holiday rep wages.

There's no obligation to make hard and fast plans, but you should be wary of falling into the trap of planning to save and travel and somehow never making it out of that stop-gap job. Having said that, once exams, teachers and careers advisers are a distant memory, it can sometimes be easier to work out for yourself just what you fancy doing and where you want to go. (The beaches in Tahiti are nice. Go on. You deserve it.)

The harsh facts of life are that pre-university, a year without obligation feels like freedom and opportunity; post-graduation, it's called unemployment. If you have the chance of travelling now, go for it. And turning up at college with a bit more experience under your belt than a few A-levels will make you an irresistible source of fascination to greener, doe-eyed contemporaries. Well, maybe.

 Contact

- **Raleigh International**
  - www.raleigh.org.uk

- **Project Trust:**
  - www.projecttrust.org.uk

- **STA**
  - www.statravel.co.uk

- **BUNAC**
  - www.bunac.org

- **Gapyear.com**
  - www.gapyear.com

- **Timebank**
  - www.timebank.org.uk

- **The Foreign and Commonwealth Office**
  - www.fco.gov.uk

■ Budgeting

The one certainty about student life is that once you've spent what will seem like eons getting hold of your cash, you'll find that it trickles through your fingers like sand – and pretty fine sand at that. So having expended so much effort in getting hold of what precious money you can, you've now got to redouble that effort, just to keep it. If you want to avoid serious problems, you've simply got to learn to keep track of your outgoings and try to make your income and spending balance as much as is possible.

The first step is to **know what's going on with your finances**. It might sound simple (patronising even), but if you have no idea of what is going into and out of your account, you are much more likely to overspend and get into trouble by, for example, running out of money for rent before the end of term. Not only that, but being financially astute is fast becoming a necessary life skill – as financial products such as pensions and mortgages multiply and change – so you may as well get some practice in while you're a student.

The first thing to do is **add up the money you have from loans, jobs, parents and so on**. Divide this by the number of weeks you will be at university. Most universities teach for 30 weeks a year, but in practice you will probably arrive a week early and/or leave a week late, or stay in your student accommodation over a holiday, so it's best to play safe and divide your income by at least 35 weeks.

Then **make a list of all your unavoidable costs**. This will include any contribution you have to make towards fees, rent, bills, food, clothes, transport and entertainment. Always calculate for the worst-case scenario – spending more than you would hope – since most of those in serious debt are hopelessly optimistic. Ideally, you'll surprise yourself with your financial discipline.

Make a weekly budget. It may sound boring, but just about every student advice centre says this is a crucial step. It might seem a bit dull to be scribbling down details of your expenditure in a petty cash book (or on a computer spreadsheet), but it will be worth it. You will be able to see what unnecessary purchases you make and cut them out, and set aside any spare cash to do the things you really want to do (such as travel during the holidays); second, it will prove very handy if you have to go cap in hand to the bank manager seeking an extended overdraft.

Accommodation will be your biggest expense and your university should be able to give you an idea of what average accommodation – both in student and private, rented flats – will cost. Rents can start as low as £50 a week in student halls outside the capital and rise to about £110 a week for a room in a shared, privately rented flat in London. In halls, bills are usually included. In private accommodation, they are extra and average around £400 a year. If you have the option of **living at home**, do consider it.

It may not be what you had in mind when you imagined university, but a few more years at mum and dad's could save you thousands of pounds. You don't have to feel like a mummy's boy or girl just for making a financially astute choice – studying from home is an attractive option for an increasing number of students. It obviously cuts down on food and rent (assuming your family don't soak you for every penny they can), then there's the tantalising possibility of a laundry and ironing service and the feeling of being generally being looked after – a place where the food includes fresh vegetables. Studying at a university near home is the norm in continental Europe and a long tradition in big (i.e., expensive) cities in the UK, such as London or Glasgow.

If you do go away to university and if your university offers hall places to second- and third-year students as well, consider staying on – it will save you a lot of money. Admittedly, it doesn't happen very often that you have the choice, but it's worth bearing in mind.

Whatever your accommodation expenses, pay them as early as you can, before you have the chance to spend that part of your money. The last thing you need is to stare, horrified, at a final demand for rent in one hand and an empty bank statement in the other.

Food is another unavoidable expense. You'll doubtless have heard the apocryphal tale of the student who lived off porridge/noodles/biscuits for a year to save money and ended up with scurvy, so you'll doubtless want to eat healthily and should put aside at least £1,000 for the year. Shop and cook with housemates. Buy in bulk, buy basic brands (they taste almost the same), make your own meals from the basic ingredients (rather than eating pre-prepared dishes) and take a shopping list to the supermarket rather than making impulse purchases.

The cost of **course materials** will vary massively depending on what course you are studying. Science, medical and law degrees usually require expensive textbooks. Art and design students need specialist equipment that can cost several hundred pounds. Put aside at least a few hundred pounds for materials, remembering that you will need to do photocopying and continue to buy stationery throughout the year. If you can, and wherever you can, buy second-hand books or try to find the same information on the Internet. Assuming your university or college gives you free access, it can be a much cheaper way of gaining the information you need.

How much you spend on **clothing** will depend on how fashion-conscious you are. It's cheaper to aim for geek chic and buy from charity shops, and you'll end up with a much more individual look. If you're desperate for new clothes rather than 'pre-loved' then get your family and friends to get you tokens for the chain shops you love for Christmas and birthdays.

Spending on **entertainment** can vary wildly. Just as some students buy the latest designer gear and go to expensive, exclusive clubs every weekend, others make do with wearing jeans and T-shirts and drinking at the student union bar.

Whichever you are, try to be realistic about what you will spend on entertainment. By the time you get to calculate your entertainment budget, you will probably find you have already run out of money and may be tempted to imagine yourself scrimping on the fun and games to stay out of debt. This won't happen. You will go out and you need to go out to maintain and create friendships and to remind yourself that one of the reasons you are there in the first place is to enjoy yourself. So don't be a killjoy, just put aside some money for fun – at least £35 a week would be a realistic figure.

The only good news on the budget front is that, as a student, you will be entitled to **discounts** at various places. Cinemas, some pub and club chains, clothing shops and bookshops offer discounts of up to 30 per cent to students. Train and air travel is also cheaper.

■ Banks

Choose carefully

As a student, you're going to be bombarded with offers and incentives from banks, anxious to get your custom. Remember, you are a valuable property to them – they're expecting you to get a decent job so that you can be a wealthy patron of theirs for life – the old adage has it that people would rather go through a divorce than the hassle of changing banks.

But be careful about choosing your bank – as a rule of thumb, the accounts offering the biggest cash incentives or freebies usually offer the worst rates and penalties. Better to decide what's the most important thing for you and choose on that basis.

For many, that involves convenience. Most students pick the bank closest to where they live in the first year, which is fine, but remember you'll live somewhere else in your second, third and perhaps fourth year. It's also much less of an issue for telephone-based or Internet banks. So long as there's an ATM or cashpoint (which doesn't charge you), it shouldn't be a deciding factor.

For many, the **overdraft** is the biggest issue – preferably a nice big one at low cost. Most student bank accounts offer interest-free overdrafts for between three and five years. The length of time you have the overdraft is important – you're more likely to be in debt towards the end of you university career, and you don't want to be starting work with a decreasing overdraft limit. And while that overdraft limit is important, it shouldn't be the only consideration. It's easy to rack up debt beyond the bank's interest-free limit, which is why fees and interest rates for both authorised and unauthorised extensions to these limits need to be considered. These can have the effect of making a good overdraft facility suddenly look less appealing if the original limits are breached by mistake.

A bank can, for example, offer an interest-free overdraft facility of up to £2,000 for five years, with its authorised interest rate (that is, the rate on the agreed limit) set at 5 per cent above the base rate, but with an unauthorised rate (the charges when you go above the £2,000) at 22 per cent above base. It could also impose an £8.50 penalty on unauthorised borrowing and £20 for sending out a letter telling you that you have become overdrawn without agreement. Which will annoy you and no mistake.

You'd probably be better looking for a bank that can offer good overdraft buffers, which is the facility to exceed an agreed overdraft limit without getting charged either interest or fees. It might be set at, for example, £750, which gives quite a bit of leeway for those who slip further into the red on frequent occasions.

And while we're on the issue of charges, most cashpoint charges have been dropped, but it's still worth checking whether your bank will charge you for using certain cashpoints – otherwise you might find yourself paying just to take out money. You might also find yourself being charged for unpaid direct debits and charges for banker's drafts – important, as the latter are often required to pay a landlord.

Most banks charge £30 for an unpaid direct debit, although none charge for setting them up. The standard charge for a banker's draft is £10, although some offer this facility for free.

For the minority of students lucky enough to have an account permanently in credit, the interest rates paid on their balance could be a factor in their decision. Internet banks are more likely to pay generously on accounts in credit, while most of the big high-street banks pay just 0.10 per cent, which isn't very interesting at all.

Finally, it's worth checking how long the student package lasts after graduation. Many of the banks automatically transfer students to their graduate package, while others only keeps students on their package until the December following graduation.

 Also see…
www.support4learning.org.uk

■ Credit cards

Don't let the plastic get drastic

Our first advice (and second, and last) is not to bother with a credit card.

We are a nation of debtors when it comes to plastic, as the temptation proves too much for most of us, and the chances are you'll end up paying too much interest on too much debt. Yes it's convenient, but that very convenience also acts as the temptation to spend too much. Knowing that you won't have to find all of the money straight away may seem like a nice way of funding that dress-to-impress wardrobe, but in reality it's something of a fool's paradise. Much like the banks, the credit-card companies will bombard you with offers and tempting freebies, but be strong, resist.

Much of the problem with cards lies not only in their tempting ease of use, but also in their interest rates. Many cards offer 0 per cent on balance transfers and on purchases for a limited period (often six months), which may seem like good deals, but remember – these companies aren't charities. They are loaning you money and will want some interest back on their investment at some point. Most cards charge between 11 per cent and 19 per cent interest, which is not the most effective way to fund your spending when you consider the interest on an agreed overdraft, for example. Some people spend their time flitting from card company to card company taking advantage of the 0 per cent introductory periods, but you'll run out of options sooner or later – and besides, haven't you got better things to do?

And as for store cards – don't even think about it.

And if you do, forget about them again.

Store cards charge up to 30 per cent interest on purchases and if you miss a payment you will be penalised. If you think this is a good deal, are you sure you're bright enough for higher education?

And remember, if you default on your payments to credit-card or store-card companies, you could end up on bad credit lists. Credit reference agencies supply information on people who have failed to clear their debts and they pass these on to banks and building societies, etc. Which means you could have trouble getting a loan or a mortgage in the future, perhaps long after you've forgotten all about the original debt.

■ Insurance

Keeping under cover

The information pack you are given when you turn up at university will almost certainly include an offer of **student insurance**. Should you take it? The short answer is yes.

Modern young things that you are, the chances are that you've got some rather pricey items in your luggage. Your parents might have turned up with a clock radio and a Clash poster as their sole extravagance, but many among you will be arriving with a laptop computer, mobile phone, portable television, DVDs and hi-fi equipment. The average student turns up with around £3,000 worth of possessions. You may think you've got a lot less, but even if you've only got around 50 CDs in your collection, that'll still cost you around £500 to replace.

And you're pretty easy pickings. Around **one in four students will be burgled at some point** (and one in ten will be insured against it). Back in 1999, Home Office research said that student homes attract criminals 'like bees to a honey pot', and not much has change since. One in three students becomes a victim of crime whilst studying. Student accommodation tends to be in cheaper, often poorer areas of town. Cities with high student populations, such as Manchester, Leeds and Liverpool, are often burglary hotspots. On top of this, any vaguely observant burglar would have no trouble spotting a student house. Official university accommodation is clearly easy to locate, and most privately rented houses see a fresh crop of students each year.

This means that you'll be dealing with quite a serious insurance risk. Which, in turn, means you ought to **take out insurance** – or at least make sure you have some. It may be that your parents' home contents insurance already covers you or that they might be persuaded to extend their current policy to include you. If that is the case, it is still a good idea to tell your family's insurer about expensive or high-risk items, such as laptop computers, mobile phones, bikes, musical instruments and sports equipment, which may need to be specified on the policy.

Even if your parents lack the extra cover, their policy may still insure 'items temporarily away from the home' against fire, flood and theft during a break-in.

This basic cover has limitations, however. There's usually a condition that your belongings will be covered at your term-time address only if you take them home in the holidays. It's unlikely to cover stuff lost or stolen on the way to and from university, or mobiles and laptops taken outside your room. And it is almost certain to exclude claims for 'walk-in' theft by people who enter your room without breaking in. The other downside is that if you have to claim, it is your parents who will lose their no-claims bonus. Which might make you less than popular.

Students in halls of residence should check if they are covered by a block policy provided by their university. In a case like that, you may only need top-up cover for a bike or an expensive computer.

But if you do have to take on your own insurance, you'll probably be better off going to one of the specialist insurers, like Endsleigh, or the bigger companies. Wherever you go to get a quote, always find out precisely what is covered and where – some policies only apply to the student's room or to shared areas, such as a common room or kitchen.

Before you do anything else, you also need to take stock of your belongings. Work out how much your possessions are worth and try not to underestimate the value. Decide, too, whether you will be leaving your things at university during the holidays. If this is the case, you will usually need extra cover.

And watch out for large excess bills, too. The excess is the sum of money you have to pay before the insurer coughs up. So if you are claiming for the loss of something worth £300, you may have to pay the first, say, £50. The higher the excess you have to pay, the more risk you are taking over from the insurer. So even though the premiums are likely to be cheaper, if anything were to happen to your belongings you could end up bearing more of the cost of replacing your possessions than you would like.

Premiums are generally more expensive in rented accommodation – with rates set at up to five different levels of risk – yet one of the few things people insure is the deposit many students hand over to landlords at the beginning of an academic year. The NUS estimates that around 35,000 students will have their deposits withheld each year – often a substantial sum and often borrowed. Check if your policy does, or could, cover this. And check, too, if larger items are included. Sometimes you may have to take out a separate policy for larger items such as bikes. In high-risk areas of London, a £500 bike can cost students £80 a year to insure.

 Also see…

www.good2bsecure.gov.uk

■ TV licence

Don't try to get by

Many students take a TV along with them to university. Fewer of them get a licence.

If you live in shared accommodation and one among you has a licence, then you're OK, but once that person moves out, then the licence goes with them, since it belongs to the person, not the household.

If you live in a traditional hall of residence, all of those who have a TV in their study bedroom will need to have a licence unless there is only one TV set available in a communal area. If you do not, you risk being fined £1,000. If you live in what are known as 'cluster flats' (blocks of accommodation where the residents share communal facilities, including a lounge area), then unless the college has provided the set, the tenants are responsible for buying the licence. If you share a house, the TV Licensing Authority insists that if the property is divided into bedsits (and that in its view can include any property where there are locks on the bedroom doors) then you may have to get an individual licence if you have a set in your room.

If you don't have a licence, you may get away with it, but not all of you will. TV licence inspectors like to keep busy in halls of residence and student areas in towns, because the catch rate is pretty high. If you get a visit and you don't have the documents, they will leave a notice, telling you to get one sharpish, with a rather short gap in which you must take action. If you fail to do so, they will start criminal proceedings, with a hefty £1,000 fine the worst outcome.

And buying a licence (at a mere £121) is pretty simple – you just pop down to the post office (where you have to pay in full) or you can arrange quarterly direct debit or a monthly payment plan by calling 0800 328 2020 or visiting **www.tv-l.co.uk**. If you move, you can take the licence with you, but you have to inform the licensing people.

2 Earn while you learn

■ Working in the real world

Much as you'd prefer not to join the ranks of the wage slaves quite yet, around three quarters of you will roll up your sleeves at some point in your university life and take up the sort of low-paid job that most of your non-student peers wouldn't go near, just for the sheer joy of extra cash.

You may be harbouring dreams of swimming in money once you graduate, but while you're a student you are at the bottom of the food chain. You'll hear about other students starting up dotcoms, writing witty novels or doing turns as lap dancers and making oodles of cash, but the chances are that (for a variety of reasons) you'll be doing something far more mundane, like waiting on tables, handing out leaflets or selling ice-cream.

Whatever you end up doing, think about it carefully before you take on anything. Yes, you may be short of cash – but you're studying in the hope of getting good qualifications. So don't blow it just for the sake of a few extra quid, which you'll squander on some dumb alcopops promotion night anyhow.

Most students find that doing paid work adversely affects their studies – they miss lectures, fall asleep during them, skip essays and end up with worse qualifications than they had hoped or expected. This is the very worst form of short-term planning.

If you're still convinced, it's probably better to go for a job with regular shift patterns, so you know when you'll be working and can organise your study around it. It's also a smart move to arrange time off – or to give up work for a bit – in the run-up to exam periods, where stress levels are likely to be a little high, even without the added hassle of clocking on.

Finding a job shouldn't be too difficult: even the least resourceful of students can cock an eye at the ads in the newsagent's window. But if you're considering a job – and this applies more to vacation work – which could give you a leg-up come graduate recruitment time, it's a wise move to have a browse around your careers service, employment service or university job shop. Many big employers offer internships or summer placements that give an insight into the less grubby (we're not talking morals here) world of graduate work. No washing-up gloves required.

The National Association of Student Employment Services has a website which not only gives you lots of handy-dandy employment advice but also lists all the student jobshops in the UK.

 Also see...

www.nases.org.uk

Whatever you end up doing, your basic rights remain the same, whether you're jet-setting or dish-washing.

Minimum wage

The phrase 'minimum wage' does warn you that you're not going to be living the high life, but it's an important safeguard – an employer cannot get away with paying you less than £4.10 an hour if you're aged 18 to 21, or £4.85 if you're older. Be warned: this can include tips that come through the payroll and doesn't cover students on a sandwich placement as part of their course. Otherwise, you must get this much: no arguments. If your boss doesn't agree, report them to the Minimum Wage Helpline: 0845 6000 678.

Know your rights

Be sceptical of all mentions of probation periods, qualifying periods and so on. There are some rights you have from the moment you start work, whether part-time or full-time. The minimum wage is one; you are also entitled to a payslip; to working-time limits; to paid holidays (see below); to be paid the same as colleagues in equivalent jobs; to work in a safe environment; and to be protected from harassment and discrimination.

After a month, your employer will have to give you a week's notice – although the same applies to you, so no moonlight flits. After two months, you should have seen a written contract setting out your terms and conditions (if you haven't seen one – and around 40 per cent of students in casual jobs never do, according to an NUS survey – don't assume that no contract exists; you still have all the rights listed above).

Taking a break

You might be accomplished in the art of the all-night essay-fest, but your employer can't expect the same level of desk-bound devotion from you in the workplace. You can refuse to work more than 48 hours a week (and don't even think about nearing that if you're working during term-time). You also can't be made – even with bribes of free Pro-Plus – to work more than 13 hours in one day. And if you're working for six hours or more in a row, a break of 20 minutes is your right. Enough time for a sandwich and a quick crossword, at least.

Holidays

Remember them? They're what you used to have between terms at school; the time you now spend serving milkshakes to teenagers who still get them. Even though university vacations are now primarily a means of clearing study out of the way for a few weeks so you can get down to some serious overdraft repair, don't assume you're not entitled to a little time off.

Recent changes to working rules now state that all employees are entitled to four weeks' holiday a year, paid at the normal rate (pro-rata, of course, for part-timers). If you work regularly for the same boss, it's worth investigating whether you can take the odd day here and there.

Taxes, forms and other inconveniences

And no, you don't need to be studying for a maths degree for this bit. In the current tax year, which ends on 5 April, you can earn up to £4,475 without paying any tax. If your fabulously well paid skivvying takes you over this amount, you will have to pay tax on the difference. Similarly, you will only have to pay National Insurance contributions if you earn more than £89 a week. These will be niftily lifted straight from your pay packet by your employer, so if you don't want to be taxed – that is, if you're sure you won't earn enough, not that you just don't fancy it – you'll need to fill in **form P38(S)** when you start (get it from your employer).

You'll need to give a new employer the **P45** from your previous job; if you've not worked before or have inexplicably managed to lose track of your P45, fill in a **P46** (again, from your employer). This should set you up, tax-wise. It does happen, of course, that tax is deducted wrongly. This is terribly annoying, but get in touch with the tax office and they will sort it out.

International students

Overseas students on courses of six months or more are usually allowed to work up to 20 hours a week during term-time; it's unlimited in university vacations.

 Contact

- **Minimum Wage Helpline**
  (t) 0845 6000 678

- **Tax and National Insurance**
  (↗) www.inlandrevenue.gov.uk

- **TUC Know Your Rights Helpline**
  (t) 0870 600 4882

- **TUC/NUS advice for students**
  (↗) www.tuc.org.uk/tuc/rights_student.cfm

- **Rights in the workplace**
  (↗) www.troubleatwork.org.uk

3 Tax

If you're going to work, that opens you up to issues of taxation. As sure as anything, if you're going to start earning, the government is going to want a piece. The only thing to do is stop moaning and get used to it. You'll be paying tax in some form or another until you die, anyhow...

In principle, you are not in any special position regarding income tax or National Insurance, although there is one important point you need to keep at the back of your mind – LEA grants, most other educational grants and scholarships, most research awards, the student loan, and grants from the Access to Learning Fund do not normally count as taxable income. So, as a general rule, you will not have to pay income tax or National Insurance on your student support.

Once you start earning on top of that, of course, that's when the taxman gets interested. You will be charged income tax on all assessable income (income from all sources not subject to tax exemption) received during a financial year (6 April to following 5 April) at the following rates:

> **Income tax rates for 2004/5:**
> * 10 per cent starting rate on the first **£2,020** of taxable income
> * 22 per cent basic rate on taxable income between **£2,021** and **£31,400**
> * 40 per cent higher rate on taxable income above **£31,400**.

However, every person resident in the UK has a personal allowance, which makes things more complicated, but in a good way. The allowance is the amount of yearly income on which you do not have to pay tax and is deducted from total taxable income before the rate bands above are applied.

There may also be other tax allowances you can claim, depending on your personal circumstances, although being married is no longer one of those – the married couple's tax allowance was abolished in 2000.

Tax allowances for 2004/5

- Personal allowance: **£4,745**
- Blind person's allowance (additional): **£1,560**

Still not get it? Try this:

Alice earns £10,000 in the year. She pays no tax on the first £4,745 of this, 10 per cent on the next £2,020 and 22 per cent on the remaining £3,235. This means her total income tax for the year is £913.70 (i.e., £202 + £711.70).

Sponsorships and scholarships are not usually taxable as long as they do 'no more than support a student during a period of study', in the words of the Inland Revenue. If you are required to work in a company or organisation and their sponsorship is part-payment for this, you should contact the Inland Revenue for appropriate guidance.

If you're lucky enough to have savings tucked away, you should already know that banks and building societies have to deduct income tax from interest payments before these are actually credited to your savings account. However, if you do not believe your income over the course of the year will exceed your personal allowance, you can fill out **form R85** and give this to your bank or building society, who will pay the interest without deduction of tax. If tax is deducted from your interest when you are not due to pay any, or if the tax deducted is more than you are due to pay, you can claim the tax back by completing **form R40**. Both forms are available from the Inland Revenue.

If you have some rather significant savings, then tax on savings income that exceeds your personal allowance is paid on a similar basis to income tax for earnings; however, the basic rate is slightly lower. This won't be an issue for many of you, but for the sake of completeness:

Income tax rates on savings for 2004/5

- 10 per cent starting rate on the first £2,020 of taxable income
- 20 per cent basic rate on taxable income between £2,021 and £31,400
- 40 per cent higher rate on taxable income above £31,400

And should you be a real little tycoon and earn **dividends on shares**, these are also taxed – at 10 per cent up to the basic rate limit of £30,500 and then at 32.5 per cent for any amount above that. If you have shares in a company, when you get your dividend it should be accompanied by a tax credit voucher, which shows the amount of the dividend payable and the amount of the tax credit that goes with that dividend. 'Dividend income' for tax purposes is the dividend plus the tax credit.

The tax credit is not tax deducted on your behalf, but rather represents the fact that the company paying the dividend has paid tax on the profits used to pay the dividend. The tax credit, which is 10 per cent of the dividend income, can be set against your tax liability on the dividend. Put another way: as some tax has already been paid on these earnings the amount you have to pay is reduced accordingly.

Is that an issue for any of you?

For more information on getting your interest without tax being deducted, and about claiming tax back, see **www.inlandrevenue.gov.uk/taxback**. There are links to forms R40 and R85 and the booklet *A Guide for People with Savings*. If you want to contact an Inland Revenue Office, visit **www.inlandrevenue.gov.uk** or call 0845 302 1455.

■ Paying your income tax

If you earn money on top of your student support, you'll be paying your income tax in one of a number of ways:

- If you are **employed** in the 'normal' way, you'll pay under the Pay As You Earn (PAYE) system, where tax is deducted by your employer from each wage payment.

- If you are **self-employed**, you should pay under the self-assessment scheme. You will need to pay assessed tax in two instalments, due on 31 January and 31 July. Assistance and advice on the process of self-assessment, the records you should keep and on how to fill out the form is available from the Inland Revenue website at **www. inlandrevenue.gov.uk** or from the self-assessment helpline 0845 9000 444.

The issue now is, **should you be paying tax?**

If you work during the holidays, you would normally expect to have tax deducted at source under PAYE. However, if you will not earn more than the balance of your personal allowance, you should ask your employer to complete the Inland Revenue **form P38(S)**, which enables them to pay your wages without deducting any tax.

If you work in term-time in the evenings or part-time, then you are required to complete **form P46** instead. However, you may have to complete a tax return at the end of every tax year to ensure that your total taxable income has not exceeded your personal allowance.

If you are on a placement, then any wages paid to you during periods of practical experience are taxable as earned income, subject to the usual tax-free allowances. However, if any wages are paid to you for periods spent at college, they are normally taxable but can be tax free if the following concession can be claimed:

- You are enrolled in college for at least one academic year

and

- Attendance at college amounts to at least 20 weeks' full-time instruction within that academic year

and

- Your level of earnings, including lodging or subsistence allowances, does not exceed £7,000 (excluding any fees paid by the employer) or the level of earnings does not exceed the amount which you would have received from a Research Council studentship or any other grant fixed by the DfES, whichever is the higher.

If the qualifying period is less than one year, the above amounts should be reduced on a pro-rata basis.

Support and benefit

If you are receiving **Income Support** and **Housing Benefit**, these are not normally taxable. Jobseeker's Allowance (JSA) is taxable, though it is not deducted while benefit is paid, but instead reduces the refund you might otherwise receive through pay-as-you-earn (PAYE) when you return to work. Leaflet **IR60** (available from the Inland Revenue) provides further information on taxation of JSA as it relates to students.

All those who earn above a certain amount contribute to the social security system via National Insurance, and paying into the scheme will entitle you to a range of benefits later in life, including the state pension.

National Insurance Contributions (NICs)

The Inland Revenue National Insurance Contributions Office (NICO) keeps the records for everyone's contributions throughout their working life, and should issue you with a National Insurance number on your sixteenth birthday. Employers will need a number in order to comply with taxation law, and if you do not have a number you will find it difficult to secure employment. In the event you have lost your number or do not otherwise have one (if you are an international student who is permitted to work in the UK, for example), you must contact your local Department of Work and Pensions office, or, in Northern Ireland the Department for Social Development.

If a new number must be issued, the process can take several weeks to be completed, but in the meantime it is possible for an employer to use a temporary number until such time as a permanent one is issued. This is formed by the letters TN in front of your date of birth in the form DD/MM/YY and then either M or F to indicate male or female. For example, a male born on 16 January 1979 would have the temporary number TN 16 01 79 M.

You will not be required to pay National Insurance on normal student financial support, but you will be required to pay if you are earning and your pay exceeds the earnings threshold of £91 a week (or £395 a month). If so, you must pay Class 1 (earnings-related) contributions. Your employer deducts these from your wages, and the rate of contribution for 2004/5 is 11 per cent of all earnings above the £91 a week threshold, but below £610. All earnings above £610 a week incur a 1 per cent rate of contribution. For example:

> Bob earns £700 a week. He pays no National Insurance on the first £91. He pays 11 per cent on the next £419, and then 1 per cent on the remaining £90. Therefore, his weekly National Insurance contribution is £46.99.

If you are **self-employed**, you have to pay flat-rate Class 2 contributions of £2.05 for each week of self-employment if your income exceeds £4,215 in the 2004/5 tax year (if you have a lesser income you must apply for an exception). You also have to pay Class 4 contributions of 8 per cent on profits or gains between £4,745 and £31,720 and 1 per cent on any amount above this, but only if you are resident in Britain for income tax purposes. Contact the Inland Revenue for more details.

If you are a research student you should check if you are liable for Class 1 or Class 2 contributions if you are paid for teaching or demonstrating.

Placement students are liable to pay Class 1 contributions while receiving wages/salaries for periods of work experience. Additionally, you are liable for these contributions while at college if you continue to receive wages.

No contributions are payable if you are under the age of 16 or over pensionable age, although you may have to apply for an exemption if your earnings would otherwise attract NICs.

Your entitlement to the state retirement pension is dependent on you having paid NICs at a set level for a set number of years during your 'working life' (usually about 90 per cent) for the full pension. Reduced rates are possible but NICs must still have been made at the correct rate for at least 25 per cent of that time.

However, if you have not or believe you may not have fulfilled this qualification you can pay voluntary contributions in order to make up the 'missing' years. These contributions are paid at a flat rate under Class 3; the rate for 2004/5 is £7.15 a week.

You can only preserve your entitlement to the state pension, widow's and bereavement benefits in this way and if you do not have a recent record of employment you cannot gain access to short-term benefits (for example, income-based Jobseeker's Allowance, Incapacity Benefit and Maternity Benefit) by paying Class 3 contributions.

Before committing yourself to expensive voluntary contributions, you should consult your local NI Contributions office or call the Retirement Pension Forecasting Scheme on 0845 3000 168 to ascertain your likely pension at retirement age. Most younger students will not suffer a reduction to any pension entitlement by not paying NI during their studies, as they will have sufficient time after completing full-time education in which to qualify for full pension rights.

 Contact

- **Inland Revenue**
  - ⌲ www.inlandrevenue.gov.uk

  Get leaflet 1R60:
  Income Tax and Students

- **TaxationWeb**
  - ⌲ www.taxationweb.co.uk/articles

  Produces online information on
  tax issues for students

Tax credits

There are two types of tax credit: the **Child Tax Credit** (**CTC**) and the **Working Tax Credit** (**WTC**), which also has a childcare element. You can apply for the tax credits, just the same as any grown-up, if you meet the eligibility requirements. As the tax credits system has now replaced parts of the student support system, it is very important that you apply for any tax credits to which you are entitled.

You can claim **Child Tax Credit** if you:

☑ are a lone parent with one or more children

☑ are in a couple and have one or more children

☑ are responsible for at least one child who is 'normally living with' you

☑ have children who are either under 16 or under 19 and at school

☑ are not subject to immigration control.

You are able to claim Working Tax Credit if you:

☑ are 16 or over, have children and are working at least 16 hours a week

☑ are 16 or over, have a disability and are working at least 16 hours a week

☑ are over 25 and working 30 hours a week

☑ are 50 or over, have been claiming Income Support, Jobseeker's Allowance or Incapacity Benefit for at least 6 months, and are now working more than 16 hours a week

☑ are not subject to immigration control.

If you are eligible for WTC, you may also be able to claim for childcare if you:

- are a single parent, working at least 16 hours a week, and incurring 'relevant childcare charges'

- are a couple, both working at least 16 hours a week between them, and incurring childcare costs

- are a couple, one working and the other incapacitated, incurring childcare costs.

Tax Credits are composed of various elements, which are cumulative.

Child Tax Credit	Maximum annual amount	Weekly equivalent
Family element (per family)	£545	£10.45
Baby element (per child under 1 year old)	£545	£10.45
Child element (per child)	£1,625	£31.25
Disabled child element (per child in receipt of the Disability Living Allowance [DLA] or registered blind)	£2,215	£42.60
Severely disabled child element (per child in receipt of the highest rate care component of the DLA)	£890	£17.10

Working Tax Credit	Maximum annual amount	Weekly equivalent
Basic element (16 hours)	£1,570	£31.15
Lone parent or couple element	£1,545	£29.70
30 hour element	£640	£12.30
Disability element	£2,100	£40.35
Severe disability element	£890	£17.10
50+ return to work element (16 to 29 hours)	£1,075	£20.65
50+ return to work element (30+ hours)	£1,610	£30.95

To calculate the total entitlement, all qualifying elements should be added together.

Whether you receive the maximum rate of tax credits or a reduced rate will depend on your income (joint income if you have a partner).

As a student, the following will be classed as income for the purposes of tax credits:

- Child Dependants' Grant (except the NHS dependants' grant)
- Adult Dependants' Grant
- Lone Parents' Grant
- Two Homes Grant
- Any part of a Career Development Loan paid for living expenses.

But the good news is that the following are not included as income when calculating your credits:

- grants for tuition fees
- the Higher Education grant

- loans from the Student Loan Company
- the childcare grant
- the school meals grant
- the travel, books and equipment grant
- the Disabled Students' Allowance
- travelling expenses
- postgraduate studentships from any research council, the British Academy or the SAAS
- social work bursaries
- NHS bursaries, dependants' allowances and travel expenses
- Access to Learning Fund grants
- hardship loans.

And if you're in further education, you're home free on:

- Education Maintenance Allowances
- Care to Learn grants
- Learner Support Fund hardship grants
- two homes allowance
- residential bursaries
- childcare bursaries.

Other forms of income, including taxable social security benefits, any wages or salary earned either as an employee or while self-employed, profits from a business, share dividends or other investment income and pensions are all counted as income when assessing tax-credit entitlement. The first £300 of income from pensions and/or investments is disregarded, you lucky things.

Non-taxable social security benefits (such as Child Benefit, Housing Benefit, Council Tax Benefit, Income Support, Maternity Allowance and Disability Living Allowance) are all disregarded too.

You can apply online or pick up an application form (**TC600**) from the Inland Revenue Enquiry Centre, Job Centre Plus, some money advice centres, Citizens Advice Bureaux or institution finance offices.

Once you're peering at the form, you'll find there's no section in which to note student income, so it should be noted in 'other'.

You should only enter that part of your student income which is assessable (go back a page or so and read it slowly). Disregarded income should not appear on the form – a confused government worker is rarely your friend. Thus, only dependants' allowances, the lone parents' grant and the two homes allowance should be entered as income – any other student income should not be entered in the form. If you are unsure what to include, ask your student union or association or your institution's student adviser for assistance.

This is a relatively new system and some students may find themselves worse off as an obviously complicated system replaces an equally complicated system and not all bases are covered. If you find you are worse off, you should apply to your institution's Access to Learning Fund to make up the difference.

 Contact

- **Inland Revenue**
  (t) 0845 603 2000
  Textphone: 0845 607 6078
  (Both helplines open seven days a week from 8 a.m. to 8 p.m.)

  (↗) www.inlandrevenue.gov.uk

■ Social security

The vast majority of full-time students are not entitled to claim three key means-tested Social Security benefits: **Housing Benefit, Income Support** and **Jobseeker's Allowance**. This exclusion includes the summer vacation period as well as term-time. Most full-time students are also unable to claim Council Tax Benefit (the exceptions are those groups of full-time students who can claim Housing Benefit). But there are exceptions...

Income Support

There are a number of exempt groups of students who are entitled to claim Income Support throughout the year (i.e., during term-time and vacations). You can claim if:

- ☑ You are under 19 and in 'relevant' education (studying at least 12 hours a week in non-advanced education, up to and including A-levels or Scottish Highers)
- ☑ You are a parent
- ☑ You are disabled and unlikely to get a job in the next 12 months
- ☑ You have no living parent and no-one acting as a parent (for example, a foster parent). If you fall under the provision of the Children (Leaving Care) Act 2000, you will be provided for by your local authority, rather than through the benefits system
- ☑ You have to live away from your parents because you are estranged, in physical or moral danger
- ☑ You are a lone parent with a child or children up to age 16. Please note that if your child or children are aged 16 or over you are not entitled to Income Support
- ☑ You're single and looking after a foster child or children up to age 16
- ☑ You're disabled, defined as:
    - ☑ You qualify for the Disability Premium or Severe Disability Premium
    - ☑ You have been treated as incapable of work for a continuous period of at least 28 weeks (two or more periods of incapacity separated by a break of no more than eight weeks count as one continuous period, as well as counting as extremely unlucky)
    - ☑ You are a deaf student who qualifies for the Disabled Students' Allowance under the Mandatory Awards or Student Support Regulations or as a postgraduate student
- ☑ You are from abroad and entered on limited leave and your funds are temporarily disrupted (this lasts for a maximum of six weeks)
- ☑ You are a refugee attending a course of English Language for 15 hours per week or more for a maximum of nine months
- ☑ You are a pensioner.

Obviously, some of these are more likely than others.

Housing Benefit

There are eight groups of students who are able to claim Housing Benefit. You can claim if:

- [✓] You are aged under 19 and following a course of further education and are liable to pay rent for your accommodation. If you live with close relatives you are unlikely to be able to claim Housing Benefit, even if they make you pay rent. Be sure to mention that when you get home

- [✓] You're a lone parent with a child or children under 19. There's probably a reason why it's a different cut-off age for children than when you're claiming Income Support, but we don't know what it is

- [✓] You are solely responsible for a child boarded out with them by a local authority or voluntary organisation

- [✓] You are a disabled person (judged by the same definitions as above)

- [✓] You are one of a couple, both of whom are students, with a dependent child or children

- [✓] You are receiving Income Support and/or income-based Jobseeker's Allowance (JSA)

- [✓] You're a pensioner who meets the conditions for award of the Income Support Pensioner Premium or Higher Pensioner Premium

- [✓] You're a full-time student and have suspended your studies due to illness or caring duties. You may claim Housing Benefit from the day after you recover from their illness or cease your caring duties until the day before the date you have agreed with the institution to return to your course, or the day before you return to your course – whichever comes first. The claim period must be no longer than one academic year. You may also claim Council Tax Benefit during this period if need be.

Jobseeker's Allowance (JSA)

Full-time students are generally not entitled to JSA. As ever, there are exceptions:

- [✓] If you are one half of a student couple with dependent children you can claim JSA during the summer holidays only, if you are available for employment

- [✓] If you are full-time student who has stopped your studies due to illness or caring duties (you may be looking after a sick relative, for example) you may claim JSA once you have recovered from your illness or ceased your caring duties and are waiting to return to your course. You can claim JSA from the day after you recover or cease caring duties until the day before you have agreed with the institution to return to your course or the day before you return to your course – whichever date comes first. This claim must be no longer than one academic year. After six months on JSA, if you are under 25 you will be required to go on to the New Deal 18–24 programme. It used to be that you could claim JSA while you were pregnant, but they no longer view pregnancy as an illness, which is a victory of sorts.

New Deal

It may be possible to study full-time under the New Deal schemes for 18–24 and 25-plus age groups. Both of these schemes have a Full-Time Education and Training Option, which could enable you to study for up to a year in order to make you more employable. Entry to these schemes is dependent on your period in receipt of Jobseeker's Allowance (JSA) – or in the case of the 25-plus scheme, receipt of JSA or its equivalent, usually Income Support. For the 18–24 scheme, you will usually need to have been in receipt of JSA for six months. For the 25-plus scheme, the receipt period is usually 18 months. Contact your local Employment Service office or Job Centre for information or visit the New Deal website: **www.newdeal.gov.uk**.

■ Part-time study

If you are studying part-time, you may still qualify for benefits. As ever, we need to get the definitions out of the way first: In England and Wales, you may be classed as part-time if:

- ☑ You are under 19 and spend 12 hours a week or less in non-advanced education

- ☑ Your course is funded by the Learning and Skills Council (LSC) or Education and Learning Wales (ELWa) and has a Learning Agreement, stating that it is 16 guided learning hours or less per week

- ☑ Your course is one of higher education and is not defined as a full-time course by your education institution.

Definitions of part-time study within further education vary across

England, Wales, Scotland and Northern Ireland. Check locally for details.

It may be possible to study part-time while claiming JSA, Income Support or Incapacity Benefit, if you satisfy the other conditions for these benefits. You may also be entitled to apply for Housing Benefit on the grounds of low income.

If you are studying a modular course you have an entitlement to JSA or Income Support and Housing Benefit while registered on a part-time basis, providing you are not repeating a module which you first studied on a full-time basis, even if you failed or did not complete that module on your earlier attempt. If you change your mode of course from full-time to part-time, you have to prove your new part-time status to qualify for these benefits.

Part-timers and JSA

To claim the JSA, you must still be available for and actively seeking work. If you're studying part-time as well as job-seeking, this will be taken into account when judging whether you qualify, since you will still need to be available for work for 40 hours a week and be willing and able to take up employment at once if it is offered. You may get away with it if you are able to arrange your study periods so that you are available for work or if you have been in receipt of the JSA or other financial support for a period of three months prior to starting the course. Check with a student adviser at the college before you start your study.

Bear in mind with all these claims for JSA, Income Support and Housing Benefit that these are means-tested and your student financial support will be counted when you make a claim.

4 Health

The easiest way to save money on health matters is not to get ill. Don't suffer physically and your wallet won't be taking the strain of prescription charges. So take our advice, keep your vest on and don't go out with wet hair, you should be OK...

■ Staying healthy

Talk to most students about their early university experiences and at some point they'll mention succumbing to a ferocious bout of 'freshers' flu'. Late nights, excessive alcohol, poor diet, new pressures and exposure to an unprecedented assortment of other people make the average first-year undergraduate a perfect target for opportunistic bugs. With any luck this will be the worst health hiccup you'll be confronted with at university, but be prepared.

Get a GP

The first thing to do is to get yourself on the books of a GP near to your accommodation. Often there will be a dedicated campus health centre where you can register, but if not, the welfare advice centre in the students' union should be able to tell you where the nearest practices are, or you can phone NHS Direct. You'll be asked for your NHS card and the details of your previous doctor, but you'll still be taken on if you don't have them.

You should also look into finding the nearest NHS dental practice, as it's very easy to forget to go for the biannual check-up (especially if your mum is no longer making the appointment for you). You certainly don't want to be in the position of not having a dentist if you start to get severe toothache. Again, the students' union welfare service or NHS Direct can help you in your search. One money-saving tip, if you're lucky enough to live in one of the big cities, is to find out if you can use the local dental school for treatment. It does mean being treated by a student (albeit one who is supervised by a fully qualified dentist), but the treatment is usually free, and with the cost expensive enough even if you aren't a full-time student it's probably the best bet.

Accidents

Over 4,000 people die due to domestic accidents each year and many of these are down to the following: impatience, carelessness, stress, fatigue, absent-mindedness, irresponsible behaviour and taking risks. If this reads like a fairly comprehensive assessment of your likely state of mind when tackling potentially hazardous tasks such as cooking, take care. It's a good idea not to use your thumb to prise open tins or try to part frozen hamburgers with sharp knives. Wires and clothing strewn on the floor can be a threat to health and safety, too, and if chilling out is your thing, be warned – there are more than 2,000 fires a year caused by candles.

 Also see…

www.rospa.com

Sexual health

While the hazards of HIV/AIDS are likely to be clear in the minds of most first years, other infections, such as chlamydia, are far less well understood. Thanks to these blind spots in students' knowledge and the usual maelstrom of sexual activity that characterises the early stages of some people's university or college life, most student unions will be eager to supply you with condoms. Some will also have dental dams and lubrication, and most will carry information on sexual health and the details of the local GUM clinic should you need a check-up.

Drugs

There is not the space here to repeat specific information about individual drugs and their effects. Just remember:

- Avoid using drugs alone
- Do not buy drugs from people unknown to you
- Tell people what you are taking
- Avoid drug cocktails or using drugs in combination with alcohol
- Don't attempt to drive following drug use.

Meningitis

According to the National Meningitis Trust, widespread immunisation against the 'C' form of meningitis has encouraged worrying complacency among students towards this potentially lethal disease. The vaccine is only 80 per cent effective and there's no inoculation for the more common 'B' strain. The meningococcal bacteria are present at the back of the throat in one in 10 people, but students in their first weeks of university have proved twice as vulnerable to it, compared with the general 18 to 25 population. Welfare services usually provide little cards listing symptoms and helpline numbers, small enough that you can keep it in your wallet or purse.

Mental health

At some time during your first year you may feel down. One piece of research estimates that as many as six out of 10 freshers experience some depression and that between 10 and 20 per cent of students will seek psychiatric help during the course of their studies.

The worst time is the period immediately after students return from their Christmas holidays. By then the honeymoon with student life is over. You may have woken up to the fact that, while you were hot stuff at school, there are many seemingly more intelligent and confident people around you at college. If that is the case and your social circle isn't very supportive, see your tutor, your students' union welfare officer, your GP, or call the local NHS Direct centre, any one of whom can help you identify the problem and help you find the help you need.

Contact

- **NHS Direct** (t) 0845 4647

- **Drinkline helpline** (t) 0800 917 7377

- **Brook Advisory Centre** (t) 020 7617 8000

- **Sexwise** (t) 0800 282930 (under 19s)

- **British Pregnancy Advisory Service** (t) 08457 304030

- **Sexual Health Line** (t) 0800 567 123

- **Release (drugs and legal advice)** (t) 020 7729 9904

- **National Drugs Helpline** (t) 0800 776600

- **The Samaritans** (t) 08457 909090

- **National Schizophrenia Fellowship** (t) 020 8547 6814

- **Depression Alliance** (t) 020 7633 0557

But supposing that fails and you do end up ill or injured, be aware that most treatment for UK residents is free under the National Health Service, but some charges are levied on the public for NHS services and treatments. These include:

- prescriptions
- dental treatment
- wigs or fabric supports
- sight tests
- glasses (spectacles) or contact lenses.

All claims are dealt with by the Patient Services department of the Prescription Pricing Authority (PPA) based in Newcastle upon Tyne (call 0845 850 0030 or visit **www.ppa.org.uk**).

As a student, you are not automatically exempt from paying such health costs unless you fall into one of the categories defined below. But even if you don't, you may be exempt from certain costs or you may apply for a remission certificate under the 'Low Income Scheme', which allows part or all of these costs to be waived, depending on your income. Look, it's complicated, read on...

Full exemption from NHS charges

Under the current system there are a number of possible ways in which, as a full- or part-time student, you may be exempt from paying any of the charges above. To fall into those categories, you must:

- ☑ receive Income Support (IS) or income-based Jobseeker's Allowance (JSA)

or

- ☑ receive Child Tax Credit (CTC) or CTC and Working Tax Credit (WTC) or WTC with a disability element; and your gross income be less than £14,600 per annum

or

- ☑ be in receipt of a war disablement pension and your prescription be in relation to that disability.

(Some of these are more likely than others.)

Free prescriptions

You can claim free prescriptions if you fall into one of the following categories:

- ☑ you are aged under 16 or under 19 and in full-time education
- ☑ you are aged 60 or over
- ☑ you are aged under 25 (Wales only)
- ☑ you have a low income
- ☑ you are pregnant or have given birth within the last 12 months
- ☑ you have a specific medical condition.

The following conditions are eligible for payment exemption on medical grounds:

- a continuing physical disability that prevents you from leaving home except with the help of another person
- epilepsy requiring continuous anti-convulsive therapy

- a permanent fistula, including caecostomy, ileostomy, laryngostomy or colostomy, needing continuous surgical dressing or an appliance
- one of the following conditions for which specific substitution therapy is essential: diabetes mellitus; myxoedema; hypoparathyroidism; diabetes insipidus and other forms of hypopituitarism; forms of hypoadrenalism (including Addison's disease); myasthenia gravis.

Free sight tests

You can qualify for a free sight test if you fall into one of the following categories:

☑ you are under 16 or under 19 and in full-time education*

☑ you are aged 60 or over

☑ you have a low income*

☑ you are registered blind or partially sighted

☑ you have been prescribed complex lenses*

☑ you have diabetes or glaucoma

☑ you are over 40 and are the parent, sibling or child of someone who has diabetes or glaucoma

☑ you are a patient of the Hospital Eye Service.*

* If you are in these groups, you will also be eligible for a voucher towards the cost of glasses or contact lenses if they are prescribed after a test.

Free dental treatment and dentures

You can qualify for dental treatment or dentures if you fall into one of the following categories:

☑ you are aged under 18, or under 19 and in full-time education

☑ you have a low income

☑ you are pregnant or have given birth within the last 12 months

☑ you are a patient of the Community Dental Service.

In addition, if you are a resident of Wales aged under 25 or over 60 you are eligible for free dental checks.

Free wigs and fabric supports

You can qualify for free wigs or fabric supports if you fall into one of the following categories:

- ☑ you are aged under 16 or under 19 and in full-time education (see section 2 below)

- ☑ you have a low income (see section 4 below)

- ☑ you are a hospital in-patient when the wig or fabric support is provided.

Free milk and vitamins

You are eligible for free milk tokens if you fall into any of the following categories:

- ☑ you are pregnant and you or your partner receives income support, income-based JSA or pension credit guarantee credit

- ☑ you have a child under five and receive IS, income-based JSA or child tax credit and have an income for tax-credit purposes of £13,480 or less

- ☑ you have a disabled child of school age who does not go to school because of their disability.

In addition, you are eligible for free vitamins if you fall into any of the following categories:

- ☑ you are pregnant or breastfeeding a child under one, and receiving IS or income-based JSA

- ☑ you have a child under five and get IS, income-based JSA, or receive child tax credit and have an income for tax-credit purposes of £13,480 or less.

You are eligible for help with the costs of travel to hospital or other NHS facilities if you are in any of the groups who are fully exempt from NHS charges or if you fall into any of the following categories:

☑ you have a low income

☑ you are a patient at a genito-urinary medicine clinic more than 15 miles from your home (or 5 miles if your required attendance is weekly)

☑ you live in the Highlands and islands of Scotland or the Isles of Scilly.

■ Getting the exemptions

You can get the exemptions you've just read through if you fall into the categories, but how do you claim?

Students under 19 in full-time education

To claim the exemption from NHS prescription charges, you need to sign the declaration form on the back of your prescription.

To claim a free sight test, you need to sign the optician's form before your test. If, following the sight test, glasses or contact lenses are prescribed, vouchers for these will be issued in the following circumstances:

- if glasses or contact lenses are required for the first time
- if there is a new prescription
- if the old glasses have reasonable wear and tear
- if you are under 16 and you have damaged your glasses without the recourse to insurance cover.

To claim free dental treatment, you must tell the dental receptionist before your treatment that you think you are exempt from charges. You will need to complete a form at this point.

Pregnant women and new mothers

To claim free dental treatment and prescriptions, you will need to apply for an exemption certificate on **form FW8**, which should be available from your midwife, health visitor or doctor.

Students with a low income

Your average student will not qualify for exemption from most NHS charges, unless they are on a low income. The Department of Health means-tests you to determine whether you qualify for either a full or partial exemption certificate. The means test is roughly based on the Department for Work and Pension's 'applicable amounts' for Income Support (pages 160–61), but there are some differences.

Unlike student loans, the income assessed is only your own and your partner's or spouse's where appropriate. Your parents' income is not assessed. However, any money given to you by your parents may be taken into account when assessing eligibility.

If your calculated **income** (see below) is less than or equal to your **requirements** (again, read on), you will receive a full exemption certificate (an **HC2 certificate**). If your income exceeds your requirements – i.e., you are deemed to have excess income – you may receive a 'partial remission' of charges for services (a **HC3 certificate**), dependent on the level of excess. An HC3 certificate will include the following:

- dental charges which are higher than three times your excess income
- a voucher for glasses or lenses, reduced by an amount equal to your excess income
- where your excess income is lower than the cost of a sight test, the cost is reduced to your excess income.

Applications for help under the low-income scheme should be made to the PPA on an **HC1 form**, available from post offices, benefits agencies, some GPs surgeries, many student union advice centres or on request at **www.ppa.org.uk/ppa/low_income.htm**.

The PPA will require evidence of income, for example a grant/loan/bursary confirmation letter. The claim will not be processed until this evidence has been received and verified.

Calculating income

To qualify for help as a student on a low income, you must have less than £8,000 in property, savings or other assessed income and capital. This rises to £12,250 if you are aged 60 or over and £20,000 if you live in a residential or nursing home. It is calculated from the following:

• **Regular maintenance**
Regular maintenance, including child support, part-time employment, parental or spousal contributions towards maintenance and Initial Teacher Training salaries count as income. As a general rule, income will normally be taken into account in the week in which it is paid, subject to a weekly disregard of £5, £10 or £20 depending on your circumstances.

• **Lump-sum payments**
Lump-sum payments (for example, one-off payments from Access to Learning Funds or Initial Teacher Training Shortage Subject Area Schemes) are treated as capital.

• **Loan income**
The student loan is treated as income over a 52-week period, except where you are in your final year or taking a one-year course (in which case it is divided by the number of weeks between the start and end of that year of the course). In their calculations the PPA will use the maximum rate of student loan available to you, including (where appropriate) any means-tested element – even if the applicant has chosen not to take this amount and/or where any or all of the means-tested element has not been granted. As with the assessment for Income Support, the loan is treated as **notional income**, as the Government believes that it is the primary source of public support to students and therefore should be fully exhausted before further support is granted. Any amount granted for extra weeks' attendance is also included.

A standard disregard of £605 (2003/4 rates) for books, equipment and travel is deducted from the loan amount.

• **Career Development Loans**
If you have taken a CDL for a specific purpose (for example, the purchasing of equipment), it will be disregarded. However, if you have taken it to pay for general maintenance, it will be treated as income over the period for which it is payable.

- **Grant income**

Grants, scholarships, studentships or bursaries (including postgraduate Research Council awards and means-tested NHS bursaries) will be apportioned over the period for which they are payable (for example, a grant may be payable over 38–9 weeks). For students who started their higher education before September 1998, a standard travel and equipment disregard will be applied as for student loans above.

The following grants and allowances are disregarded when looking at your income:

- Disabled Students' Allowances
- Grants for tuition fees
- Grants for childcare
- Education Maintenance Allowances
- Parents' Learning Allowances
- Welsh Assembly Learning Grants.

Non-means-tested NHS bursaries, the Lone Parents' Allowance, and dependants' grants are treated as income, taken into account over 52 weeks. Initial Teacher Training salaries will be treated as income over the period for which they are payable – usually nine months.

- **Access to Learning Funds**

In general, if the payment is for living costs it is taken into account in full if it counts as capital or with up to a £20 a week disregard if it counts as capital. If the payment is for other costs, it is disregarded. For example, an FE learner-support-fund grant solely for childcare costs is disregarded.

Calculating requirements

So, that's your income worked out. The second part of the equation is the requirements, which are based on those used for calculating the applicable amount for Income Support, and include the following elements:

- Income Support personal allowances
- Income Support premiums – including those for disability, as long as either you or your partner have been incapable of work for 28 weeks or more; mortgage or rent liability can be included here if you qualify for a severe disability premium

- rent, less any Housing Benefit
- Council Tax, less any Council Tax Benefit
- mortgage – both interest and capital
- capital payments on loans secured on your home and loans taken out to adapt a home for the needs of a disabled person.

If you've ploughed your way through all that, then you deserve to have this repeated as you try and make sense of it all:

> if your calculated **income** is less than or equal to your **requirements**, you will receive a full exemption certificate (**an HC2 certificate**). If your income exceeds your requirements – i.e., you are deemed to have excess income – you may receive a **partial remission** of charges for services (**an HC3 certificate**), depending on the level of excess. An HC3 certificate will include the following:
> - dental charges which are higher than three times your excess income
> - a voucher for glasses or lenses, reduced by an amount equal to your excess income
> - where your excess income is lower than the cost of a sight test, the cost is reduced to your excess income.

Refunds

If you pay for an NHS treatment or service that you could have got free or at a reduced cost, you can claim back the costs within three months of payment (or longer at the discretion of the PPA if there was a good reason for late application). Prescriptions are refunded on **form FP57**, which you must get when you pay for the prescription at the pharmacy or dispensing chemist. A bilingual version, **WP57**, is available in Wales.

Other costs are refunded on **form HC5**, available from post offices, benefits agencies and some GPs' surgeries.

If you wish to have your cost refunded on the basis of low income, but do not already have an **HC2** or **HC3** certificate (see above), you should send a completed **HC1** form to the PPA with the **HC5** form. Yes, it's that simple...

Pre-payment certificates (PPCs)

If you are likely to need a lot of prescriptions but are not exempt from payment under the above categories, you may reduce the cost by buying a pre-payment certificate. A holder of a PPC does not have to pay any further charges for prescriptions for the duration of the certificate, regardless of how many are required.

A four-month certificate will save money on more than five prescriptions, while a year-long certificate will save money on more than 14 prescriptions. Applications can be made by post on form **FP95**, available from chemists and most GPs' surgeries. This should be sent to the address on the form. Applications can also be made by telephone on 0845 850 0030 or online at **www.ppa.org.uk**.

Currently a four-month PPC costs £33.40 and a 12-month PPC costs £91.80. Prices usually rise in April each year.

Overseas students

Asylum seekers

If you are an asylum seeker or the dependant of an asylum seeker and receiving support from either the National Asylum Support Service (NASS) or a local authority, you are eligible for full exemption from NHS charges. If you are supported by NASS, you should contact NASS on 0845 602 1739 (9 a.m. to 4.45 p.m. Monday to Friday) to obtain an **HC2** (exemption) certificate, while those supported by local authorities should apply for exemption using an **HC1** form, available from post offices and benefits agencies.

Other overseas students

If you are an overseas student on a course lasting longer than six months (or any length in Scotland), you qualify for NHS treatment and help with NHS charges on the same basis as UK residents. In addition, any family members with you in the UK will also qualify.

Health benefits are not classed as public funds and therefore will not affect your immigration status.

If you are an overseas student on a course lasting less than six months in England, Wales or Northern Ireland, you can get emergency treatment, treatment of certain communicable diseases and compulsory psychiatric treatment free through the NHS, but other treatments and services will incur a charge. You are, therefore, strongly advised to take out adequate medical insurance for the duration of your stay in the UK.

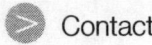 Contact

For bulk orders of HC1 forms (for example, for student union advice centres):

- **Department of Health Stores**
  PO Box 777, London , SE1 6XH

  (t) 08701 555 455

  (f) 01623 724524

  (e) doh@prolog.uk.com

- **Prescription Pricing Authority – Patient Services**

  (t) 0845 850 11 66

  (↗) www.ppa.org.uk

  The PPA will advise students on low-income-scheme claims.

- **UKCOSA**
  9–17 St Albans Place, London , N1 0NX

  (t) 020 7288 4330
      Helpline: 020 7107 9922 (1 p.m.–4 p.m. Monday to Friday)

  (f) 020 7288 4360

  (↗) www.ukcosa.org.uk

  UKCOSA provide advice and information for overseas students, including guidance on healthcare benefits.

5 Housing

You can get too cynical about student housing – it can be excellent, even suitable for grown-ups. University-owned accommodation is often (but by no means always) very good – often functional and inelegant, but usually with all the facilities you'll need: cooker, fridge, roof, the lot.

There's no getting away from it, though – some housing deemed 'suitable for students' is mouldy, draughty or suitable only for amphibians.

It shouldn't be. All housing, by law, has to meet certain standards if it is to be rented. Know those standards and know your rights, and you're halfway there.

■ The joys of staying put

It might be that you have a long-term partner who cannot leave their job, you may have children or you may be reluctant to stray too far from the family nest, your old mates or the football team that has reached the Premiership for the first time in your life. There are lots of reasons to choose a university close to home, but an increasingly common one is the fact that it enables you to stay right where you are.

University is a costly business, as you know, and staying at home to go to your local university is an increasingly popular choice. It's cheaper, obviously. Even if you pay a contribution to your mum it's not going to bear any resemblance to what it would cost you in the open market – and besides, no landlord cooks you your favourite dish when you need cheering up. Or does your washing. It may be that there are one or two more restrictions on your social life than you'd hoped for, but that might be healthier and help you actually get the work done – which is, after all, at least one of the reasons you're heading to university in the first place.

Studying at a university near home is the norm in continental Europe and a long tradition in big (i.e., expensive) cities in the UK, such as

London or Glasgow. So if you think it'll do for you, you'll know what to expect, you know the landlord, so you can skip much of the rest of the chapter and head back to the one which tells you how much money you've got coming your way.

■ Happy campus

For most first-year students your choice is generally between living in university-owned accommodation (often known as halls) or going for the privately rented option – usually in a shared house.

That's the norm at any rate, but some universities suffer a shortage of accommodation and cannot find a place for everyone. Each year the newspapers will have a story about some students somewhere who are living it up in some posh hotel because the university halls weren't finished in time. More usually, there will be students who miss out on a place in halls because there simply isn't enough room.

But for the majority your university will have a place for you or will help you find one. If you're heading to a campus university or one with its own halls of residence, our advice would be to take up the offer and 'live-in' in your first year. They can be soulless concrete boxes, sure, and you can end up living next to the dweeb with the poster of a tennis player scratching her bottom on his wall, but the chances are you will make some great mates and always have a door to knock on when you need a drink/shoulder to cry on/essay to borrow.

Remember, though, that it may not be for everyone. If you value your privacy or would find hordes of drunken students dragging their comatose chums round the building for hilarious pranks at 3 a.m. rather offensive, then you could find halls rather annoying.

And whatever you do, have a **look at the accommodation before you apply**. Visit the university on an Open Day if it is at all possible and don't rely on brochure photographs of pretty people enjoying sunny days – the chances are that those people left ten years ago, taking the sun with them.

But halls are generally safe, which is one of the most important things. The university has a duty of care to you – it's in their interests to keep you safe and well, so the building will be safe, with working fire alarms and regular gas safety checks.

You will, of course, pay for this, but the rent is (usually, but by no means always) reasonable and will often include some bills and the council tax – which cuts the hassle considerably.

Most universities also have accommodation adapted for **disabled students**, usually integrated into the main accommodation buildings, but in limited numbers. If you have special requirements, let the university know as soon as you get a confirmed place, to give them every chance to meet your needs. The university will almost always do everything they can to help, which makes private accommodation a much less attractive proposition – there are no laws to compel private landlords to make adaptations to their properties.

Universities also tend to have a very limited amount of accommodation for families and long-term partners – if that forms part of your living requirements, you'll need to check your chances of getting suitable university accommodation before you apply.

Most universities have more than one set of halls on offer. They will vary in cost, usually according to the size of the room, en-suite facilities, etc. The main choice that you will probably need to make is whether you choose catered or self-catered halls. If your culinary skills stretch to little more than cheese on toast, catered halls are likely to be the best choice. But don't expect haute cuisine – you'll get more than your share of lasagne and bolognese.

As estate agents will be telling you for the rest of your life, location is fundamental. Would you rather escape the campus bustle or would you prefer to roll out of bed five minutes before your lecture starts? Visit the different locations, check out the public transport and work out how long it would take you to get to uni in the mornings.

It can be tempting to opt for the most expensive room in halls, complete with your own bathroom and all the mod cons. This is ideal if you fancy spending your first year in luxury, but they are also pretty pricey, and do not guarantee you a better time. You can pick the facilities, but not your neighbours – you could be surrounded by trainspotters, nerds or (even worse) people from a different year. Find out from the university accommodation office if you will be living with your year peers before you sign anything.

Most importantly, you should visit the halls and get a feel for them before you sign anything. Just looking at a brochure will not give you the full picture. Have a look around the common rooms, bars and dining rooms. Speak to students that live there and get an honest opinion.

■ Going private

Going straight into private rented accommodation in your first year can be harder work. You might need to find flatmates and you will have to take more responsibility for bills, legal matters and safety. On the up side, you can choose where you live and who you live with. Private renting is usually for second and third year students who have had enough of abiding by hall rules (or have been lobbed out by the university, which needs to make space for the next intake). Going private gives you more freedom and independence – but with these come washing, cleaning, cooking and bills.

And, of course, there's the harsh reality that some of the clichés about student housing are based on truth – a recent survey found that 50 per cent of students living in private rented accommodation reported damp in their homes; 40 per cent had mouldy walls; 16 per cent had vermin infestations; and, perhaps most worryingly, 50 per cent had never seen a copy of a gas safety check certificate. Seek advice from your student union housing office if you are not confident that you are getting a good deal. It's crucial that you know your rights.

And one final point: most landlords are absolutely fine, honest and trustworthy, but trading standards officers (in a summer 2004 report) said that a 'significant' number of landlords withheld deposits at the end of term and charged oodles of cash to replace old items with new ones, even when they were worn out through 'reasonable wear and tear'. They also charged excessively for late payment of rent.

While some of this will be blatant cheating, some of it might be covered in the contract you naively signed. This makes it tricky if you want to wriggle out of it, but it's worth remembering that contracts are only deemed enforceable if they are fair under law. So it might be that you are being held to a contract that isn't actually legal. If you're having serious problems, contact your local trading standards office.

Where to look for a house

There are many sources that you can use to help you find the right house. The first place that you should go to for advice is your university accommodation office. They should have listings of private sector estate agents and can advise you on the best course of action. Universities should have a register of private sector agencies and properties that they recommend in the area. Many now also post these details on the university websites. Most websites will allow you to browse details of various properties, so you can house-hunt without even leaving your chair.

But there's no substitute for shoe leather – visit every student-letting agent in town and poke your nose in every nook and cranny in every flat and house that you can. Compare rents, locations, standards and walking distance to the lecture theatre/lab/pub – and whatever you do, refrain from panicking and taking the first house you see.

Here are some standard checks you should do:

- ☑ Check external features of the house for problems like rotten timber, broken guttering, blocked drains, cracked walls, etc.

- ☑ Have a thorough check of all the internal features in every room

- ☑ Are the facilities suitable for the number of people who will be sharing?

- ☑ Is the furniture in a good state of repair?

- ☑ How is the property heated?

- ☑ Is the house free of damp and mould?

There are also many safety issues that you should take note of when looking at the house:

- ☑ Ask the landlord to show you the gas safety certificate. They should also be able to prove that it has been inspected by a CORGI-registered engineer within the last 12 months

- ☑ Are there adequate smoke alarms and do they work properly?

- ☑ Are plug sockets free from damage?

- ☑ Are windows and doors properly secure?

- ☑ Are the exits such that you could escape in the event of a fire?

Although helpful, university accommodation offices don't always carry out stringent checks on the letting agents on their lists. The **National Approved Letting Scheme** (**NALS**) provides students and parents with guidelines for finding digs. As well as being available to offer tips and advice, NALS is also a voluntary accreditation scheme for letting agents. All members have to meet a set level of service. NALS insist on formal tenancy agreements, and they check that your agent has client money protection. This will ensure that your much-needed student loan cash won't just disappear into a dodgy landlord's back pocket.

> Contact

⌐ **National Approved Letting Scheme** www.nalscheme.co.uk

⌐ **Association of Residential Letting Agents** www.Arla.co.uk

⌐ **Citizens Advice Bureau** www.Adviceguide.org.uk

Deposit

Getting your deposit back when you leave a flat can be difficult. Most landlords are fair (honest), but others see the deposit as a windfall bonus. And if you go to college or university a long way from home, you may be particularly vulnerable, as an unscrupulous landlord can take advantage of the fact that any complaint has to be dealt with from a distance.

The best way to protect your deposit at the end of your tenancy is to start taking precautions at the beginning. When paying a deposit, ask your landlord for written confirmation of what it is meant to cover, and get a receipt. **Ask for an inventory** and draw one up yourself if one isn't provided. Make sure that any damage that's already there (cigarette burns, stains, breakages, etc.) is noted. If the wallpaper or paintwork is in bad condition, make a note of this as well. Send a copy of your annotated inventory to your landlord. He won't thank you for it, but it may come in handy.

If there is any damage, take photographs, preferably with a camera that marks the date automatically. Get a friend to witness and sign the photographs. Show them to your landlord and ask him/her to agree with you that things are not in perfect condition.

While you are there, do both of you a favour and **look after the landlord's property**. You have a duty to behave responsibly and if anything does go wrong, such as the toilet starting to leak or a tap starts dripping, try to minimise any damage and tell the landlord about the problem as soon as possible.

Replace things if you break them. If in doubt about the replacement, check with the landlord. If you undertake any repairs or replacements, tell the landlord in writing what you have done and keep a copy of your letter. You should also clean regularly – especially things like cookers and toilets. The longer you leave them, the harder it is to get them clean.

Ask for receipts for all the rent payments you make.

Unless you intend to leave on the last day of a fixed contractual term, you should give your landlord a minimum of four weeks' written notice, ending on a rent day, when you know that you are leaving. Even if it is the end of a fixed term, it is good practice to give notice that you do not intend to stay beyond the end of the contract.

Clean thoroughly and ask the landlord to come and inspect. Make sure everything in the inventory is still there. Go round the property carefully with the landlord, and ask if s/he can see any problems, so that you can put them right before you go. Have a friend present as well, in case you need a witness later.

Pay all the bills. Tell your gas, electricity and water suppliers the date you are moving and ask for final accounts. The landlord might want to see proof of payment before they return your deposit.

Make sure the place is really immaculate. Once you are convinced, go round with a friend and again take photographs. If your friend then signs and dates the pictures when they are developed, they will provide evidence in case of a dispute. Get into the habit of taking photos at the beginning and end of a tenancy. Your current landlord may not cause any problem, but a later one might.

As you leave, return your keys and get a receipt. Ask the landlord to let you have the deposit as soon as possible.

Deposit withheld?

First of all, are you sure you deserve to have your deposit returned? Different people have different standards, and while you may think it's OK, a landlord might have reasonable grounds to think you've left the place looking like a pigsty. But if you know you are in the right and have the evidence, write to the landlord asking for your deposit back or the reason for withholding it, and ask for a written response within seven days. Tell the landlord what evidence you have.

Some landlords have joined the **Tenancy Deposit Scheme**, where any disputes about deposit returns are investigated independently. You will have been told when you first moved in if your landlord/agent is a member. If you dispute how much of the deposit they are withholding, contact the Tenancy Deposit Scheme at:

Independent Housing Ombudsman Ltd
Norman House, 105–109 Strand, London WC2R 0AA

(t) 0845 601 1200   (e) tds@ihos.org.uk

If all else fails, you may need to start legal action against your landlord. Most deposit-return cases are dealt with in the small claims courts and are quite informal – and you will usually have to present your case yourself. If you are not confident, consider taking someone along with you to help, and get advice first. It is important to prepare your case carefully – the judge has to be convinced.

The court will not charge an allocation fee for claims of less than £1,000. This means that you can begin the proceedings without charge, assuming you are claiming less than £1,000. The only fee that you will have to pay is if the court actually makes a ruling in the case – and that will usually be deducted from the payment that is awarded.

If you have a credit card and access to the Internet, you can actually start your court action online through **www.courtservice.gov.uk**. As well as giving a full explanation of the process, there is a facility for starting money claims online, and you are guided through the procedure step by step. You can make mistakes and undo them or draft, save and return at a later date.

Alternatively, you can start by visiting your local county court. The staff cannot advise you on the merits of your claim, but there are excellent leaflets available and they will help you fill in the forms and explain the process.

Rental contracts

Some questions you need to ask yourself before you sign a rental contract:

- ☑ Is it an individual agreement or a joint agreement?
- ☑ Are you sharing all or parts of the premises with the landlord?
- ☑ Are you sharing parts of the premises with others who are not part of your household?
- ☑ Does the contract state when the tenancy commences and when it ends?
- ☑ Does the contract state how much rent is to be paid and for what period of time?
- ☑ Have you paid a deposit? If yes, do you have a receipt?
- ☑ Has the landlord provided an up-to-date copy of the inventory?
- ☑ Have you paid, or been asked to pay, a retainer?

- ☑ Have you been given the landlord's full name and current address?
- ☑ Do you know how to contact the landlord/agent in an emergency?
- ☑ Is there a provision for you to give notice to quit before the agreement comes to an end? If so, how much notice is needed?
- ☑ Does the agreement specify that the tenants are responsible for all utility bills, including water?
- ☑ Does the agreement state who is responsible for carrying out any repairs?
- ☑ Does the agreement mention any financial penalties that the landlord may make, i.e.,for non-payment of rent?
- ☑ Does the agreement mention that a charge will be made for undertaking an inventory once the agreement has come to an end?

Before you sign anything, there are some things you really should be clear on...

Individual or joint agreements

With an individual agreement the person named is liable for only their single share of any rent, bills or other costs. Joint agreements mean that everybody who is named as a tenant can be held liable, either as part of the group or individually, if your housemates do a runner.

Sharing all or some parts with the landlord

This could affect your legal status, which in turn might make it easier for the landlord to evict you. It does not have to be the landlord who lives in or shares the property; it also covers members of their family. If in doubt, seek legal advice.

Retainers

Some landlords will ask students to pay a retainer in order to guarantee the property remains available before the tenancy agreement commences. Sometimes this takes the form of payment of half-rent over the summer. Although such practices are not illegal, they are regarded as bad practice. Don't pay these unless there is a very severe housing shortage in your area and you're getting desperate.

Quitting the agreement early

Technically known as a break-clause. Although some landlords include these, they are not common. They can also have implications if it is a joint contract, as it will mean everybody will have to agree to leaving the property early, which is not always going to be the case. If such a clause is included, it normally states how much notice should be given.

Responsibility for undertaking repairs

Some landlords have attempted to write into contracts clauses that imply that the tenants are responsible for all repairs. This is not lawful. Landlords are under a statutory duty to keep their property in good repair, including supplies of heat, light and water. The external structure is also their responsibility.

Financial penalties

There have been cases where landlords write into their contracts clauses stating that should the rent be late or other charges not paid within a given time, tenants will be charged an additional daily fee. These are not illegal, but the Office of Fair Trade has ruled that the charges have to be proportionate to the loss. If you find such clauses, consult your student union.

Disputes with your landlord

Inventories

The inventory should list all the items in the property, noting their physical condition, and be as comprehensive as possible. When you're happy with this, both you and the landlord should sign the inventory and include a note on it of how much deposit has been paid. Copies should be retained by both landlord and tenant. Once an inventory has been agreed and dated by all parties it can be used as a record in case a dispute arises at the end of the tenancy.

If a landlord decides to keep a deposit unfairly, the tenants can take the case to the small claims court (or sheriff's court in Scotland) – see above, page 185. However, it is not a good idea to withhold rent due to the landlord.

Tenant vs. landlord harassment

Harassment is a criminal offence under the Protection from Eviction Act 1977. Technically speaking, the term harassment relates to acts by a landlord or their agent that are likely to interfere with the peace or comfort of the residential occupiers, or which involve the withdrawal or withholding of services reasonably required for occupation.

Harassment can take numerous forms and although a prosecution is possible for any one act, it is more likely that a legal case would be built on the basis of a number of acts that form part of an overall campaign of harassment. As well as landlords and their agents, you might be subjected to harassment from so-called third parties. These include co-tenant(s), neighbours, local youths and anyone who is targeting students for crime. If this is the case, you should get in touch with your local **Tenancy Relations Officer** (based at the local authority).

Grounds for possession

Landlords can repossess their property by citing what are known as grounds for possession. These apply to both **assured and assured shorthold tenancies**. However, while at the end of a fixed-term agreement on an assured tenancy a landlord has to supply any one of the grounds in order to gain repossession, for an assured shorthold no grounds need to be given.

There are a total of 17 grounds and they are divided into mandatory (on which the court must order possession) and discretionary (on which it may order it). For more details, see your **Welfare Officer**.

Illegal eviction

This occurs when a landlord evicts or attempts to evict you from all or part of your home without following the required legal procedure. In extreme cases this can involve landlords changing the locks or throwing your property out into the street. It's usually less dramatic than that, though.

What a landlord has to do to ensure they are not acting illegally depends on the status of the occupier. Most students living in shared houses should be given notice to quit, an automatic ground for possession and a court order. Unprotected occupiers (which includes students living in halls of residence) should be given notice and a court order will be needed. Students who live with a residential landlord and share the facilities are excluded occupiers and only need to be given notice to quit.

Illegal eviction is a criminal offence and is covered by the **Protection from Eviction Act 1977**. This gives local authorities the power (but not the duty) to investigate such incidents. So, as with cases of harassment, students should contact the Tenancy Relations Officer (based at the local authority) through their student union.

■ Location, location, location

It may be too late now, and you may already be ensconced in your little student town, but if you're still brooding about choosing, it's worth remembering that the cost of living is not the same across the country.

If money is going to be a real and constant headache, it might be worthwhile heading for one of the many splendid institutions where rent, beer and pizza don't cost the earth. And if that is the case, there's one very basic rule that holds up pretty well: **north** = **cheap; south** = **expensive**.

In some London institutions you can pay around £90 a week for self-catering accommodation; compared to Teesside, for example, where it is just over £40 a week.

While the loans available are bigger if you live in London, they are not in other areas the south-east, such as Brighton or Luton, where the cost of living is often comparable with parts of the capital.

And loans are also marginally smaller if you opt – as an increasing number of students do – to skip the rent by going to a university close to their parental home. But if that's in London or a train away from the campus, the £30 or so spent on travel a week may be better spent on rent if there's a better course in the north.

And while seemingly distant parts of the north, like Scotland or Wales, may be just the thing in rent terms, if you live in Exeter, for example, and fancy a cheap life in Paisley, remember the cost of travel up and down each term.

Beer costs vary too. A campus in the countryside may not give you access to the throbbing club life of a metropolis that other students would frequent, but it will certainly be cheaper as students opt for the subsidised pints at the union bar.

So while the north–south divide tells you something, close consideration should also be given to the cost of rent, travel and lifestyle, plus whether your location will affect your loan income and also the availability of part-time work in the area (and how much it pays). So get researching.

Rooms in university-owned halls: average cost per week (£)

Most expensive		Cheapest	
Durham University	95.67	University of Teesside	41.08
SOAS	95.34	University of Paisley	45.58
University of Exeter	91.16	University of Wales, Lampeter	45.65
City University	89.04	Lancaster University	47.00
King's College, London	86.92	University of Bradford	49.73
Saint Mary's, Belfast	86.44	University of Ulster	49.81
University of the Arts	86.16	Bolton Institute	50.00
Royal Holloway, London	85.52	University of Salford	50.71
University of Reading	85.00	New Hall, Cambridge	51.57
Goldsmiths College	84.99	Dartington College of Arts	51.62
Queen Mary, London	84.12	University of Wales, Swansea	51.64
Writtle College	83.90	Loughborough University	51.82
Glasgow College of Nautical Studies	81.56	University of Wales College, Newport	51.83
St Hilda's College, Oxford	80.98	University of Plymouth	53.30
University of Westminster	80.01	Bradford College	54.27
University of Edinburgh	79.37	North East Wales Institute	56.22
		University of Glamorgan	56.23

Source: NUS survey, summer 2004. Excludes institutions with fewer than 200 rooms.

6 Council Tax

The council tax is a combination of a property and personal tax with an emphasis on property. Each household is issued with a bill based on the value of the property and the number of adults living there – unless you live in Northern Ireland, where council tax doesn't apply.

You'll be pleased to know that the subject of council tax liability and students can be complex. If you are a part-time student it is relatively simple as you are treated like any other citizen. In other words, you are liable to pay, although you can claim council tax benefit if your income is low enough. Full-time students as a rule are exempted from council tax, but if you are a student and have lived with a non-student in any period before 1 April 2004, there is a possibility that you are liable for council tax due in that period.

As ever, the rules depend first of all on the definitions of your student status. There are three definitions of full-time students for the purposes of proving that you are exempt from council tax:

Full-time students in further or higher education.

A full-time course is defined as one that lasts for at least one academic year. You should have to attend for at least 24 weeks a year and at least 21 hours a week. This includes undertaking work experience, but if the length of time you are on work experience exceeds the time you're deemed to be actually studying, then it will not be treated as a full-time course of education.

Students under 20 in non-advanced education

For council tax purposes, you are said to be undertaking a 'qualifying course of education'. The main conditions are that you are under 20 years of age, studying on a course up to and including (but not above)

A-levels (or Highers in Scotland), Ordinary National Certificate or Ordinary National Diploma and you are normally required to study for twelve hours or more a week. The course should last for at least three months and cannot be a correspondence course or work-based training.

Foreign language assistants

This requires you to be registered with the Central Bureau for Educational Visits and Exchanges.

For the first two of these definitions, you should obtain a certificate from the educational institution to prove that you are a full-time student. You may need this for your local authority as evidence – it's generally the only acceptable proof of student status.

In most cases, full-time students are exempt from payment of the council tax, but since council tax is property-based, the exemptions actually apply to the buildings, not the people in them. So, in effect, it is the buildings that must be exempt. Read on and all will become clear...

■ Exempt properties

For students, there are three categories of exempt dwellings:

Halls of residence

The council tax regulations use the term 'halls of residence' as a category of exempt property, but the term is not defined – it applies to accommodation provided predominantly for students and which is either owned or managed by an educational institution or by a body established for charitable purposes only. The NUS views this as including accommodation provided for students and their families. Thus family accommodation that fulfils one of the other criteria above should be exempt from council tax liability – but that's not absolute and could be challenged.

Dwellings occupied only by students

This refers to property occupied by one or more residents, all of whom are students. Thus every house or flat where every adult resident is a student is an exempt dwelling. This applies during term-time and also during any vacation when you are a freeholder, leaseholder, tenant or licensee of the property and previously occupied it as term-time accommodation or intend to do so.

If you intermit or intercalate (i.e., take time away from your course), your status can cause some confusion, with some local authorities insisting that intercalating students should not be regarded as students for the purposes of council tax. But the current general stance is that intercalating students remain students and therefore exempt. Again, it's not beyond challenge.

Dwellings left empty by students

This refers to dwellings that are now empty and the 'owner' (who holds the freehold, leasehold or has a tenancy of at least six months), is now a student. For example, if you have a disability and you have had a house specially adapted for your use, you might want to return to live in that property when you cease to be a student, so it is left empty while you attend your course elsewhere. In order for the house to be included within this category of exemption, you should have become a student within six weeks of the last day of occupation, and you should have continued to be a student throughout the period since then.

Given these various categories of exempt dwellings, most full-time students will not have to pay council tax. However, if you are or were living with non-students the situation becomes somewhat more complex, and it is possible that you will be required to pay council tax for periods prior to 1 April 2004. If the council tries to charge for tax for a period before April 2004 or if you feel that some of the murkier interpretations above have gone against you unfairly, then get in touch with your local NUS.

■ Discounts

The system of discounts is based on the number of adult residents in a property. The basic council tax bill assumes that a minimum of two adults is resident – and all single-person households are entitled to a discount of 25 per cent.

There are circumstances in which a property containing more than one adult can be eligible for the single person discount. Certain groups of people can be 'disregarded for the purposes of discount', which means that their presence as residents of a property will be ignored. Those included on the ignored list include full-time students, student nurses, youth training trainees and apprentices.

Therefore, if you are a full-time student and there is only one non-student in your household, they should receive a 25 per cent discount on their bill. Which means it's their round.

Council Tax Benefit (CTB)

Council Tax Benefit (CTB) is a means-tested benefit designed to help those on low incomes pay their council tax, but, as with most benefits, student eligibility for CTB remains limited. Those groups of students who are able to claim Housing Benefit (see pages 161–2) are able to claim CTB. If you are not eligible for housing benefit, then you are not entitled to claim CTB, regardless of your liability for the tax. Simple as that. Sorry.

However, if you are a part-time student or the partner of a full-time student, you are entitled to claim. It should be noted that the definitions of 'students' and 'full-time' and 'part-time' status are slightly different in law when referring to eligibility for CTB, compared to those used when referring to liability for council tax. Which doesn't make things any easier.

For the purpose of council tax benefit, a student is simply someone attending a course of study at an educational establishment. Full-time further education students are defined as those who have at least 16 'guided learning hours' a week, but there is no set definition of 'full-time' for students in higher education. If in doubt about your status, check with the college or university registry.

Second adult rebate
(aka alternative maximum Council Tax Benefit)

All students are entitled to claim second adult rebate, if they qualify. It applies where a second adult – either a grown-up child, relative or friend – lives within a property, but does not pay rent and is not disregarded for the purpose of discount.

This rebate will reduce the council tax bill by as little as 7.5 per cent or as much as 25 per cent, depending on the income of the second adult. However, the rules relating to this rebate are (as you may gather) complex and advice should be sought from your local student union or Citizens Advice Bureau.

Reductions for people with disabilities

There are reductions available for people with disabilities. In order for these to apply, somebody (not necessarily the claimant) who lives within the property must be 'substantially and permanently disabled'.

In addition, the property must contain one or more of the following special facilities: a room needed by the person with the disability; a second bathroom or kitchen required by the person with the disability; and/or sufficient space for the person with the disability to use a wheelchair. You can use these facilities to change the valuation band on the property (it's a property – not person – tax, remember) and reducing that band below the current allocation or (in the case of homes in bands A and B) to five-ninths of the original bill.

International students

If you are an international student, you are treated in exactly the same way as home students when it comes to liability for council tax. However, any non-student spouse or adult dependants who live with you will be treated as a 'relevant person' for council tax purposes and, provided no other non-student adults are resident, the property will be exempt.

If you have entered the UK on the condition that you have 'no recourse to public funds' you are not entitled to claim council tax benefit, and this applies equally to any partner or dependants. However, even if no such restrictions are attached to your entry into the UK (if you are a national of an EU member state, for example), entitlement to council tax benefit would only be considered if you qualified as being 'vulnerable', i.e., you are a single parent or have a disability.

Asylum seekers are not eligible for council tax benefit. However, as you should have your accommodation and other essential needs provided for you under section 95 of the Immigration and Asylum Act 1999, you are not expected to pay council tax; this liability falls upon the owner of the accommodation.

Contact

- **Office of the Deputy Prime Minister (ODPM)**
  26 Whitehall, London SW1A 2WH

  (t) 020 7944 4400

  (f) 0207 944 9622

  (↗) www.odpm.gov.uk

  Government department responsible for
  the Council Tax in England and Wales.

- **Scottish Executive**
  Finance and Central Services Department,
  St Andrews House, Regent Road, Edinburgh EH1 3DG

  (t) 0131 556 8400
     Enquiry Line: 08457 741741
     Minicom: 0131 244 1829

  (e) (enquiries): ceu@scotland.gov.uk

  (f) 0131 244 8240

  (↗) www.scotland.gov.uk/

  The Scottish Executive has responsibility
  for the Council Tax in Scotland.

- **Child Poverty Action Group (CPAG)**
  94 White Lion Street, London N1 9PF

  (t) 020 7837 7979
     Advice line: 020 7833 4627 (2 p.m.–4 p.m. daily)

  (↗) www.cpag.org.uk

  CPAG does not generally advise the public,
  but its resource centre offers information, facts
  and figures on poverty and social exclusion in the UK.

7 Dealing with debt

It may be that you've been bought this book and not read it, not checked what you can claim, not taken the advice about banks, landlords and store cards and just headed off in your own sweet way into a mountain of debt, an exhausted overdraft and credit cards worn see-through by use. We'll push aside the feeling that it serves you right and move on. Just what do you do now?

■ Don't bury your head in the sand

The first step is to sit down and be a little more realistic with yourself. Take a long, hard and honest look at all your finances as the starting point to plan the best route out of trouble. Once you know the scale of the problem, you can start to get real about the number of panic buttons you need to press.

■ Relearn budgeting

Go back to the section of this book on budgeting (pages 138–40) and re-read it. And take it on board this time. Budgeting is essentially the process where you decide if you really, really need something. No, really need it. If you do, do you need to spend that much on it? Put yourself through these little agonies each time and you'll start to learn what you can actually live without. It doesn't have to be self-denial for ever, just until you're back on your feet financially.

Talk

Debt can be stressful, so it is important to tell someone. If you cannot tell a member of your family, there are a number of charities that can help you cope, from counselling to debt management strategy.

Prioritise

Sit down and prioritise your debts. For example, meeting repayments on essential services like your rent and utility bills should be your first priority. If you are paying off a range of credit cards and store cards, you should pay off those with the highest rate of interest first. Usually the store cards. The ones we told you not to get in the first place.

Change

Switch the balance of your credit card to one that charges a lower rate of interest. You can spend all your life changing cards every six to nine months and sooner or later you'll run out of options, but if we're talking emergency measures, then it's a good idea.

You may have watched a lot of daytime TV in your time as a student and seen plenty of adverts for debt consolidation loans ('one simple payment' and such blather), but don't fall for it – more often than not, these solutions simply land you with more problems, by actually increasing the total amount you end up owing. These people aren't charities either.

Don't panic!

Despite what you may think, many companies are sympathetic to people who cannot afford repayments. Recovering debt can be expensive, so they are often willing to work out an agreement. Once you've plucked up the courage to speak to your debtors, you will, more likely than not, find them more sympathetic and flexible than you were expecting. It's in everyone's interest to find a solution. But if things are getting bad, there are places and people you can talk to...

 Contact

- **Consumer Credit Counselling Service**
  - (t) Freephone: 0800 138 1111
  - (↗) www.cccs.co.uk

- **National Debtline**
  - (t) 0808 808 4000.
  - (↗) www.nationaldebtline.co.uk

- **PayPlan**
  - (t) 0800 085 4298.
  - (↗) www.payplan.com

- **Citizens Advice Bureau**

  Office opening hours vary, so check in the Yellow Pages (or www.yell.com) for the nearest to you or get general information at:
  - (↗) www.citizensadvice.org.uk.

- **National Consumer Council**
  - (↗) www.ncc.org.uk

- **Consumers Association**
  - (↗) www.which.net

- **The Money Advice Association**
  - (t) 01476 594 970
  - (↗) www.m-a-a.org.uk.

- **Money Advice Scotland**
  - (t) 0141 572 0237
  - (↗) www.moneyadvicescotland .org.uk

- **Advice UK**
  - (t) 020 7407 4070
  - (↗) www.fiac.org.uk.

  For agencies in Northern Ireland, contact the Association of Independent Advice Centres
  - (t) 028 9064 5919
  - (↗) www.aiac.net

Credit agencies

If you find yourself blacklisted when you apply for a loan or a credit card, this may well be because you have a poor record of indebtedness in the past and these companies may feel that it would be throwing good money after bad to give you another loan. Your record of non-payment of, for example, store card debts can be held against you for up to six years and will in all likelihood be information held by a credit reference agency.

These agencies collect information from subscribing companies as to how you have managed your financial arrangements with them in the past – what your credit limit is, whether you make payments on time, whether you are in arrears, and so on. They will combine this information with publicly held information about you, such as whether you are on the electoral roll (and therefore live where you say you live), records of county court judgments, bankruptcy orders and also the number of companies who have requested information on you in the past. All of this data can be good as well as bad, so just because someone knows about you, it doesn't mean it's all bad.

And there's no need to despair. The **Data Protection Act** gives you the right to see what information is held about you. If a company is going to make a search of your credit file as part of an application you are making, they must tell you. And if you want to know what it is these companies will learn about you, then the chances are that you'll find it with one (or both) of the two main credit reference agencies in the UK:

Experian Ltd
Garden Floor, Bain House, 16 Connaught Place, London W2 2ES

(t) 020 7664 1000

(f) 020 7664 1111

(↗) www.experian.com

Equifax plc
Capital House, 25 Chapel Street, London NW1 5DS

(↗) www.equifax.co.uk

If someone refuses you credit, they must tell you which of these agencies they have used.

Assuming you're not worrying that they've got you sussed and there's no point proceeding, you should write a letter to the agency and say that under section 7 of the Data Protection Act 1998 you want them to send you a copy of the file that contains information which affects your credit-worthiness. You should include your full name and current address, as well as a list of any other addresses you've used in the last six years. There will also be a small payment of around £2 or £3 (ask them for their latest charges before you send your letter), so you'll need to enclose a cheque.

Keep a copy of your request in case it gets lost in the post, but they should reply to you within seven working days. The reply will contain a set of codes to illustrate the rankings given to your individual accounts and how they've been run. They'll make life a little easier by giving you a key to the codes as well. They may also supply some details (though not the financial ones) on people with similar names at the same address, other members of your family at that address or those who have shared accommodation with you.

If the information they hold on you is factually correct, there isn't much you can do about it. If it is wrong, then you must take steps to correct it. If you can't be bothered or if you think that dealing with such things is equivalent to fraternising with the enemy, then rest assured it will come back and bite you on the backside later. Financial life is like that.

So if the file contains details on people with whom you have no financial connection, you should ask the agency to disassociate you from them so that they no longer appear on your file. You simply have to write to them asking them to do this and explaining the reason (if, for example, it was a family member who has now left the address and has no joint commitments with you). The agency must reply to confirm whether they have corrected your file. If you don't hear from them, you can refer it to the Office of the Information Commissioner (see below).

If the file contains errors on debts that you did, in fact, pay off, then write to them in the same way, explaining your reasoning. Again, they must reply to you within 28 days to confirm whether they have corrected the file, removed the entry or decided not to change the record at all. If they refuse to change the information, you should send them a notice of correction, which they must add to your file so future searchers will see it. In the notice you can clarify a default on payments in the past – perhaps you were out of the country or ill and unable to make payments. If the agency thinks your notice of correction is not worth the paper it's written on for some reason, they can apply to the Information Commissioner for a ruling and, if the Commissioner agrees with them, it won't go in your file.

Otherwise, it will be added (and they must confirm this within 28 days) and also sent to any company that has requested a search within the last six months. You may get that loan after all.

 Contact

■ **The Office of the Information Commissioner**
Information Commissioner's Office, Wycliffe House, Water Lane, Wilmslow, Cheshire SK9 5AF

(t) 01625 545 745

(f) 01625 524 510

(e) mail@ico.gsi.gov.uk

- **Information Commissioner's Office – Scotland**
  28 Thistle Street, Edinburgh EH2 1EN

  (t) & (f) 0131 2256341

  (e) Scotland@ico.gsi.gov.uk

- **Information Commissioner's Office – Wales**
  2 Alexandra Gate, Ffordd Pengam, Cardiff CF24 2SA

  (t) 02920 894929

  (f) 02920 894930

  (e) Wales@ico.gsi.gov.uk

- **Information Commissioner's Office – Northern Ireland**
  Room 101, Regus House, 33 Clarendon Dock, Laganside,
  Belfast BT1 3BG, Northern Ireland

  (t) 028 90 511200

  (f) 028 90511584

  (e) ni@ico.gsi.gov.uk

■ Bankruptcy

You'll have heard about students declaring themselves bankrupt and thereby writing off student loans, in exchange for a period of financial purgatory. Almost a thousand students declared themselves bankrupt in 2003, more than three times the level of the previous year.

It might sound like a promising option, but it was never a good idea in the first place (you'll spend the next few years struggling to get loans, mortgages, credit cards, etc.) and the legal loophole that allowed this to happen was closed when the Higher Education Act was passed in the summer of 2004. So forget it.

Local Education Authorities and their equivalents

England and Wales

Students in England and Wales must apply for financial support through their local education authority

■ **Barking and Dagenham**
Student Support, London Borough of Barking and Dagenham, Town Hall, Barking, Essex IG11 7LU
AWARDS OFFICE
t 02082 273309
f 02082 273304

■ **Barnet**
Borough Treasurers, London Borough of Barnet, Fenella, Babington Road, Hendon, London NW4 4BS
STUDENT FINANCE OFFICE
t 02083 592233
f 02083 592233
e student.finance@barnet.gov.uk

■ **Barnsley**
Student and Pupil Support, PO Box 63, County Way, Barnsley, South Yorkshire S70 2TJ
STUDENT SUPPORT
t 01226 773595, 01226 773570
01226 773581
f 01226 773592
e SandraO'Neill@barnsley.gov.uk
louisehalford@barnsley.gov.uk
chrisstones@barnsley.gov.uk

■ **Bath and North-East Somerset**
Student Support, Bath and North East Somerset Council, PO Box 25, Riverside, Temple Street, Keynsham, Bristol BS31 1LA
STUDENT SUPPORT
t 01225 394319
f 01225 394482
e student_support@bathnes.gov.uk

■ **Bedfordshire**
Student Support, Bedfordshire County Council, County Hall, Cauldwell Street, Bedford MK42 9AP
STUDENT SUPPORT
t 01234 718400
f 01234 408010

■ **Bexley**
Student Support, Bexley Council, Hill View, Hill View Drive Welling, Kent DA16 3RY
HEAD OF PUPIL AND STUDENT SUPPORT
t 02083 037777
f 02083 194302

■ **Birmingham (LEA in pilot)**
Student Support, Birmingham City Council, Council House Extension, Margaret Street, Birmingham B3 3BU
AWARDS OFFICE
t 01213 033647, 01213 033648
f 01213 032365, 01213 034724
e studentsupport@birmingham.gov.uk

■ Blackburn with Darwen
Student Support, Blackburn with Darwen
Borough Council, Town Hall,
King William Street, Blackburn BB1 7DY
AWARDS HELPLINE
- **t** 01772 261444
- **f** 01254 698388

■ Blackpool
Student Support, Blackpool Borough
Council, Progress House, Clifton Road,
Blackpool FY4 4US
STUDENT AWARDS OFFICE
- **t** 01253 476526
- **f** 01253 476504

■ Blaenau Gwent
Student Support Service Division,
Civic Centre Ebbw Vale, Municipal Offices,
Ebbw Vale, Blaenau Gwent NP23 6XB
- **t** 01495 355412
- **e** emma.jones@blaenau-gwent.gov.uk

■ Bolton
Student Support, Bolton Metropolitan,
Borough Council, PO Box 53, Paderborn
House, Civic Centre, Bolton BL1 1JW
STUDENT AWARDS OFFICERS
- **t** 01204 333333, 01204 332135
  01204 332136, 01204 332140
- **f** 01204 332145

■ Bournemouth
Student Support Team, Education
Directorate, Dorset House, First Floor,
20–22 Christchurch Road,
Bournemouth BH1 3NL
STUDENT SUPPORT OFFICE
- **t** 01202 456267, 01202 456355
  01202 456199, 01202 456201
- **f** 01202 456191
- **e** student.support@bournemouth.gov.uk

■ Bracknell Forest
Student Finance Team, Bracknell Forest
Borough Council, Seymour House,
38 Broadway, Bracknell RG12 1AU
- **t** **A–G** 01344 354026
  H–Z 01344 354025
- **f** 01344 354146
- **e** student.finance@bracknell-forest.gov.uk

■ Bradford
Community Development and Lifelong
Learning, Student Support Service,
9 Charles Street, Bradford BD1 1DT
- **t** 01274 432639
- **f** 01274 753041
- **e** studentsupport@bradford.gov.uk
- ↗ www.bradford.gov.uk/studentsupport

■ Brent
Communication and Student Support,
London Borough of Brent, Chesterfield
House, 9 Park Lane, Wembley,
Middlesex HA9 7RW
- **t** 02089 373030
- **f** 02089 373047
- **e** students.grants@brent.gov.uk
- ↗ www.brent.gov.uk/education

■ Bridgend
Finance and Awards Section, Bridgend
County Borough Council, Sunnyside,
Bridgend CF31 4AR
STUDENT AWARDS OFFICE
- **t** 01656 642637

■ Brighton and Hove
Student Support, Brighton and Hove
Council, PO Box 2503, King's House,
Grand Avenue, Hove BN3 2SU
STUDENT SUPPORT TEAM
- **t** 01273 293603, 01273 293604
  01273 293605
- **f** 01273 293549
- **e** student.support@brighton-hove.gov.uk

■ Bristol
Student Support, Bristol City Council,
PO Box 1111, Council House, College Green,
Bristol BS99 2EZ
AWARDS OFFICE
- **t** 01179 036666
- **f** 01179 037963

■ Bromley
Education Department, London Borough
of Bromley, Bromley Civic Centre,
Stockwell Close, Bromley BR1 3UH
STUDENT SUPPORT
- **t** 02083 134094
- **f** 02083 134145

■ Buckinghamshire
Student Support Adult Learning,
Buckinghamshire County Council,
County Hall, Aylesbury, Bucks HP20 1UZ
STUDENT SUPPORT TEAM
- **t** 01296 383268
- **f** 01296 382871
- **e** studentsupportteam@buckscc.gov.uk
- **↗** www.buckscc.gov.uk/studentsupport

■ Bury
Education Department, Bury Metropolitan
Borough Council, Atheneaum House,
Market Street, Bury BL9 0SW
SENIOR AWARDS OFFICE
- **t** 01612 535676
- **f** 01612 535653

■ Calderdale
Calderdale Metropolitan Borough Council,
Student Awards Section, Northgate House,
Northgate, Halifax HX1 1UN
- **t** 01422 357 257

■ Cambridgeshire
Cambridgeshire County Council, Student
Support Service, ELH 1112, Castle Court,
Shire Hall, Castle Hill, Cambridge CB3 0AP
- **t** 01223 717942
- **f** 01223 717771
- **e** student.support@cambridgeshire.gov.uk

■ Camden
London Borough of Camden, Student
Support Office, Crowndale Centre,
218 Eversholt Street, London NW1 1BD
- **t** 020 7974 1678
- **e** awards@camden.gov.uk

■ Cheshire
Cheshire County Council: Adult Education,
Student Support Office, Goldsmith House,
Hamilton Place, Chester CH1 1SE
- **t** 01244 603 840
- **e** studentsupport@cheshire.gov.uk

■ Cornwall
Cornwall LEA, Student Services,
Camel Building, County Hall, Treyew Road,
Truro TR1 3AY
- **t** 01872 322 000

■ Corporation of London
Corporation of London, PO Box 270,
1 Bassishaw Highwalk, London EC2P 2EJ
- **t** 020 7332 1750

■ Coventry
Coventry City Council Education Service,
Student Support, New Council Offices,
Earl Street, Coventry CV1 5RS
- **t** 024 7683 1547
- **e** student.support@coventry.gov.uk

■ Croydon
Croydon Education Department, Student
Awards Section, Taberner House, Park Lane,
Croydon CR9 1TP
- **t** 020 8683 1142/51

■ Cumbria
Cumbria County Council, Education Office,
5 Portland Square, Carlisle CA1 1PU
- **t** 01228 606 060

■ Darlington
Education Department, Darlington Borough
Council, Town Hall, Darlington DL1 5QT
STUDENT AWARDS OFFICE
- **t** 01325 388807/8
- **f** 01325 388883

Denbighshire

Student Support, Denbighshire County
Council, Caledfryn, Amithfield Road,
Denbigh LL16 3RJ

STUDENT SUPPORT

t 01824 706777

f 01824 706780

Derby

Student Support, Derby City Council,
Middleton House, 27 St Mary's Gate,
Derby DE1 3NN

STUDENT AWARDS OFFICE

t 01332 716911

f 01332 716920

e student.support@derby.gov.uk

Derbyshire

Student Support, Derbyshire County Council,
County Office, Matlock, DE4 3AG

STUDENT SUPPORT OFFICE

t 01629 585350

f 01629 580350

Devon

Student Support Office, Bradninch Hall,
Castle Street, Exeter EX4 3PJ

t 01392 383981

f 01392 383904

e stusupp@devon.gov.uk

↗ www.devon.gov.uk/eal/students

Doncaster

Education Department, Doncaster
Metropolitan Borough Council,
The Council House, Doncaster DN1 3AD

t 01302 737218, 01302 737174
  01302 737176

f 01302 737223

Dorset

Student Support Service, Education
Directorate, Dorset County Council,
County Hall, Dorchester, Dorset DT1 1XJ

t **A–C** 01305 224368
  D–L 01305 224419 / 224146
  M–S 01305 224167 / 224145
  T–Z 01305 224300

f 01305 224499

e studentsupport@dorsetcc.gov.uk

↗ www.dorsetcc.gov.uk/studentsupport

Dudley

Student Support, Dudley Metropolitan
Borough Council, Westox House,
1 Trinity Road, Dudley DY1 1JQ

STUDENT SUPPORT OFFICE

Mrs J Wagstaffe / Miss S Whorton

t 01384 814237, 01384 814228

f 01384 814216

e studentsupp.ed@dudley.gov.uk

↗ www.dudley.gov.uk/council
  /educate/StudentSupport.htm

Durham (LEA in pilot)

Education Departments, Durham County
Council, County Hall, Durham DH1 5UJ

STUDENT AWARDS OFFICE

t 01913 833222

f 01913 860487

e student.support@durham.gov.uk

↗ www.durham.gov.uk

Ealing

Student Support, London Borough of Ealing,
Ground Floor Perceval House,
14–16 Uxbridge Road, Ealing W5 2HL

STUDENT SUPPORT

t 02088 255555

f 02088 255151

e studentsupport@ealing.gov.uk

↗ www.ealing.gov.uk/services
  /education/student

East Riding of Yorkshire

County Hall, Cross Street, Beverley
HU17 9BA

STUDENT FINANCE

t 01482 394680

f 01482 394684

e Student.Awards@eastriding.gov.uk

East Sussex (LEA in pilot)

Student Support, East Sussex County
Council, PO Box 4, County Hall, St Anne's
Crescent, Lewes BN7 1SG

STUDENT SUPPORT OFFICE

t 01273 481000

f 01273 481539

e student.support@eastsussexcc.gov.uk

↗ www.eastsussexcc.gov.uk/edu
  /student_support/main.htm

- **EMA–Wales**
  - t Information line: 0845 601 3636

- **Enfield**
  Education Department, London Borough of
  Enfield, PO Box 56, Civic Centre Silver
  Street, Enfield EN1 3XQ
  AWARDS OFFICE
  - t 02083 795366
  - f 02083 793243
  - e student.services@enfield.gov.uk
  - ↗ www.enfield.gov.uk

- **Essex**
  Essex County Council, The Schools Service,
  Student and Pupil Financial Support
  Services, PO Box 5287, County Hall,
  Chelmsford CM1 1LT
  - t 01245 245900
  - f 01245 245939
  - e student.support@essexcc.gov.uk
  - ↗ www.essexcc.gov.uk/studentsupport

- **Flintshire**
  Student Support, Flintshire Education
  Authority, County Hall, Mold CH7 6ND
  STUDENT SUPPORT
  - t 01352 704067, 01352 704140

- **Gateshead**
  Education Offices – Access and Lifelong
  Learning, Gateshead Metropolitan Borough
  Council, Learning and Culture, Civic Centre
  Regent Street, Gateshead NE8 1HH
  STUDENT SUPPORT
  - t 01914 333000 01914 332703
    01914 332715, 01914 332741
    01914 332742
  - f 01914 787223
  - e ChrisHegarty@Gateshead.gov.uk
  - ↗ www.gateshead.gov.uk/educ
    /studentsupport.htm

- **Gloucestershire**
  Student Support, Gloucestershire County
  Council, Shire Hall, Gloucester GL1 2TP
  - t A–J 01452 425393
    K–Z 01452 425395
  - f 01452 425399
  - e edawards@gloucestershire.gov.uk
  - ↗ www.gloucestershire.gov.uk/students

- **Greenwich**
  Student Support, London Borough of
  Greenwich, Riverside House, Woolwich High
  Street, London SE18 6DZ
  - t 02089 212910, 02089 212545
  - f 02089 212984

- **Gwynedd**
  Student Support, Gwynedd County Council,
  The Council Offices, Caemarfon LL55 1SH
  PRINCIPAL AWARDS OFFICE
  - t 01286 679185

- **Hackney**
  Student Support Section, The Learning
  Trust, Hackney Technology and Learning
  Centre, 1 Reading Lane, London E8 1GQ
  - t 02088 207253, 02088 207241
  - f 02088 207252
  - e studentsupport.hackney@
    learningtrust.co.uk
  - ↗ www.learningtrust.co.uk

- **Halton**
  Halton Borough Council, Education and
  Social Inclusion Directorate, Student
  Services Team, Grosvenor House, Halton
  Lea, Runcorn WA7 2WD
  - t 01928 704370, 01928 704375
    01928 704367
  - e education.student.services@
    halton-borough.gov.uk

- **Hammersmith and Fulham**
  Student Support, London Borough of
  Hammersmith and Fulham, Town Hall,
  Kingstreet, London W6 9JU
  STUDENT SUPPORT AND BENEFITS
  - t 02088 469911
  - f 02085 765501

- **Hampshire (LEA in pilot)**
  Student Support, Hampshire County Council,
  The Castle, Winchester SO23 8UT
  STUDENT SUPPORT
  - t 0196 284 7970, 0196 284 7980
  - f 0196 287 7462
  - e ctc2info@hants.gov.uk
  - ↗ www.hants.gov.uk/finance/stusupp

■ Haringey

Student Support, London Borough of
Haringey, 48 Station Road, Woodgreen,
London N22 4TY

STUDENT AWARDS

t 02084 891923
f 02084 891945
↗ www.haringey.gov.uk

■ Harrow

Student Support, London Borough of Harrow,
PO Box 22, Civic Centre, Harrow HA1 2UW

STUDENT SUPPORT UNIT

t 02088 635611
f 02084 270810

■ Hartlepool

Jonathan Gent, Student Support Officer,
Education Department, Civic Centre,
Victoria Road, Hartlepool TS24 8AY

t 01429 523770
f 01429 523750
e jonathan.gent@hartlepool.gov.uk

■ Havering

Student Support, London Borough of
Havering, The Broxhill Centre,
Broxhill Road, Romfod RM14 1XN

SENIOR AWARDS OFFICE

t 01708 433870
f 01708 433685

■ Herefordshire

Student Support Service, Educational
Services Directorate, PO Box 73,
Worcester WR5 2YA

t A–Do 01905 765904
　　 Dr–Ke 01905 765905
　　 Kh–Ri 01905 765908
　　 Ro–Z 01905 765907
f 01905 765660
e studentsupport@worcestershire.gov.uk
↗ www.worcestershire.gov.uk
　　 /studentsupport

■ Hertfordshire

Student Finance, Hertfordshire County
Council, County Hall, Hertford SG13 8DF

STUDENT FINANCE MANAGER

t general enquiries: 01992 555772
　　 A–K 01992 556755
　　 L–Z 01992 556716
f 01992 588596
e studentfinance@hertscc.gov.uk
↗ www.hertsdirect.org/studentfinance

■ Hillingdon

Student Support, London Borough of
Hillingdon, Civic Centre, Uxbridge UB8 1UW

SENIOR AWARDS OFFICE

t A–D 01895 250854
　　 E–K 01895 250855
　　 L–R 01895 250243
　　 S–Z 01895 250425
f 01895 250878

■ Hounslow

Student Services, London Borough of
Hounslow, Civic Centre, Lampton Road,
Hounslow TW3 4DN

t general enquiries: 02085 832811
　　 general enquiries: 02085 832817
　　 Aaa–Con 02085 832812
　　 Coo–Harp 02085 832813
　　 Harr–Lad 02085 832820
　　 Lae–Pate 02085 832810
　　 Patf–Sand 02085 832815
　　 Sane–Zzz 02085 832814
f 02085 832613

■ Isle of Anglesey

Student Services, Isle of Anglesey County
Council, Education and Leisure Department,
Glanhwfa Road, Llangefni,
Anglesey LL77 7EY

t 01248 752930, 01248 752980
f 01248 752999
e erwed@ynysmon.gov.uk
　　 wwxed@ynysmon.gov.uk

Isle of Wight

Student Finance – Directorate of Education and Community Skills, Isle of Wight Council, County Hall, Newport, Isle of Wight PO30 1UD

STUDENT SUPPORT

- **t** 01983 823465
- **f** 01983 826099
- **e** student.finance@IOW.gov.uk
- ↗ www.eduwight.iow.gov.uk/students

Isles of Scilly

Student Support, Council of the Isles of Scilly, Town Hall, St Mary's, Isle of Scilly TR21 0LW

STUDENT AWARDS OFFICE

- **t** 01720 422537
- **f** 01720 422202

Islington

Student Support Section, Regeneration and Education Department, Islington Council, Laycock Street, London N1 1TH

- **t** 02075 275700
- **f** 02075 275565
- **e** studentsupport@islington.gov.uk

Kensington and Chelsea

Student Support, Royal Borough of Kensington and Chelsea, Town Hall, Hornton Street, London W8 7NX

PRINCIPAL AWARDS OFFICE

- **t** 02073 613330
- **f** 02073 612078
- **e** student.support@rbkc.gov.uk

Kent

Student Support, Kent County Council, Bishops Terrace Bishops Way, Maidstone, Kent ME14 1AF

STUDENT AWARDS OFFICE

- **t** A/B/D/F/X/Y   01622 696570
      C/L/M/O/R/U/V 01622 696574
      H/I/N/Q/S/W/Z 01622 696576
      E/G/J/K/P/T 01622 696572
- **f** 01622 605108
- **e** student.awards@kent.gov.uk

Kingston upon Hull

Student Support Learning Services, Essex House, Manor Street, Kingston upon Hull HU1 1YD

STUDENT AWARDS OFFICE

- **t** 01482 613403
- **f** 01482 613675
- **e** studentsupport@hullcc.gov.uk
- ↗ www.hullcc.gov.uk/studentsupport /index.php

Kingston upon Thames

Student Support, Royal Borough of Kingston upon Thames, Guildhall 2, Kingston KT1 1EU

STUDENT SUPPORT SECTION

- **t** 02085 474617, 02085 474618
- **f** 02085 475235
- **e** student.support@rbk.kingston.gov.uk

Kirklees

Student Awards Section, Kirklees Metropolitan Council, Education Access Service, Upperhead Row, Huddersfield HD1 2JL

- **t** 01484 221689, 01484 221690
  01484 421691, 01484 421692
  01484 421694
- **f** 01484 416273

Knowsley

Education and Lifelong Learning Department, Education Office, Huyton Hey Road, Huyton, Merseyside L36 5YH

- **t** 01514 433258, 01514 433265
- **f** 01514 433266
- **e** hestudent.support@knowsley.gov.uk

Lambeth

Student Support, London Borough of Lambeth, Access 1st Floor, International House, Canterbury Crescent, London SW9 7QE

PUPIL AND STUDENT OFFICE

- **t** 02079 269474, 02079 269475
  02079 269622
- **f** 02079 269397

■ Lancashire
Student Support Service, Lancashire
County Council, PO Box 61, County Hall,
Preston PR1 8RJ
STUDENT SUPPORT OFFICE
- t 01772 531444
- f 01772 532862
- e student.support@ed.lancscc.gov.uk
- ↗ www.studentsupport.lancashire.gov.uk

■ Leeds
Student Support Office, Corporate Services
Department, Leeds City Council, PO Box 584,
2 Great George Street, Leeds LS2 8WJ
STUDENT SUPPORT OFFICE
- t 01132 475326
- f 01132 475320
- e student.awards@leeds.gov.uk

■ Leicester
Student Awards, Loans and Grants,
Leicester City Council, 10 York Road,
Leicester LE1 5TS
STUDENT AWARDS OFFICE
- t 01162 527855
- f 01162 339922
- e bednj001@leicester.gov.uk

■ Leicestershire
Awards, Loans and Grant Services,
Education Department, County Hall,
Glenfield, Leicester LE3 8SA
STUDENT AWARDS OFFICE
- t 01162 656376, 01162 656382
- f 01162 656400
- e studentloans@leics.gov.uk

■ Lewisham
Student Support, London Borough of
Lewisham, 3rd Floor Laurence House,
Catford Road, London SE6 4SW
PRINICPAL BENEFITS OFFICE
- t 02083 146223
- f 02083 143019
- ↗ www.lewisham.gov.uk/studentSupport
  /index.asp.

■ Lincolnshire
Student Support, PO Box 244,
Lincoln LN1 1WN
STUDENT AWARDS OFFICE
- t 01522 836595
- f 01522 516083
- e student_support@lincolnshire.gov.uk
- ↗ www.lincolnshire.gov.uk

■ Liverpool
Liverpool Direct Limited, Education Awards
Section, PO Box 2013, Liverpool L69 2DY
STUDENT AWARDS OFFICE
- t 01512 333006
- e Educ.Awards@liverpool.gov.uk

■ Luton
Student Support Manager, Luton Borough
Council, Lifelong Learning Dept Unity
House, 111 Stuart Street, Luton LU1 5NP
STUDENT SUPPORT OFFICE
- t 01582 548080
- f 01582 548454
- e educationawards@luton.gov.uk

■ Manchester
Education Department, PO Box 191,
Overseas House, Quay Street,
Manchester M3 3ST
STUDENT SUPPORT
- t A–F 0161 2347078
  G–M 0161 2347079
  N–Z 0161 2347264
- f 0161 2347004

■ Medway
Medway Student Finance Team, Education
and Leisure, Medway Council, Civic Centre,
Strood, Rochester, Kent ME2 4AU
- t 01634 332371, 01634 332379
- f 01634 332440
- e student.finance@medway.gov.uk

■ Merthyr Tydfil
Student Support, Merthyr Tydfil County
Council, Ty Keir Hardie Riverside Court,
Avenue de Clichy, Merthyr Tydfil CF47 8XD
STUDENT AWARDS OFFICE
- t 01685 724604 Students with children
  A–E 01685 724604
  F–Z 01685 724627

Merton

Student Support Section, London Borough of Merton, Civic Centre, London Road, Morden SM4 5DX

- **t A–G** 02085 453255
- **H–O** 02085 453254
- **P–Z** 02085 453257
- **f** 02085 453252
- **e** student.support@merton.gov.uk
- ↗ www.merton.gov.uk

Middlesbrough

HBS Service Middlesbrough, Student Support Team, PO Box 352 First Floor, Middlesbrough House, Middlesbrough TS1 1XH

STUDENT SUPPORT
- **t** 01642 726535
- **f** 01642 264982

Milton Keynes

Student Support Adult Learning, Buckinghamshire County Council, County Hall, Aylesbury, Bucks HP20 1UZ

- **t** 01296 383268
- **f** 01296 383871
- **e** studentsupportteam@buckscc.gov.uk
- ↗ www.buckscc.gov.uk/studentsupport

Monmouthshire

Student Support, Monmouthshire County Council, County Hall, Croesyceiliog, Cwmbran NP44 2XH

STUDENT AWARDS OFFICE
- **t** 01633 644507, 01633 644664

Neath Port Talbot

Student Pupil Support Section, Neath Port Talbot County Borough Council, Port Talbot Civic Centre, Port Talbot SA13 1PJ

STUDENT AWARDS OFFICE
- **t** 01639 763730

Newcastle-upon-Tyne

Education Office, Newcastle-upon-Tyne City Council, Civic Centre, Newcastle-upon-Tyne NE1 8PU

STUDENT SUPPORT
- **t** 01912 328520
- **f** 01912 114983

Newham

Education Offices, London Borough of Newham, Broadway House, 322 High Street Stratford, London E15 1AJ

AWARDS OFFICE
- **t** 02085 578668
- **f** 02085 578937

Newport

Student Support, Newport City Council, Civic Centre, Newport NP20 4UR

- **t** 01633 656656

Norfolk

Student Support, Education Department, County Hall, Norwich NR1 2DL

- **t A–C** 01603 222336 / 222447
- **D–J** 01603 222335 / 222444
- **K–Q** 01603 222436 / 222443
- **R–Z** 01603 222337 / 222338
- **f** 01603 222119
- **e** studentsupport.edu@norfolk.gov.uk
- ↗ www.esinet.norfolk.gov.uk/studentsup

North East Lincolnshire

Student Support, North East Lincolnshire Council, 39 Heneage Road, Grimsby DN32 9ES

AWARDS OFFICE
- **t** 01472 323323
- **f** 01472 323209

North Lincolnshire

Student Support, North Lincolnshire Council, Hewson House, PO Box 35 Station Road, Brigg DN20 8XJ

STUDENT SUPPORT OFFICE
- **t** 01724 297286
- **f** 01724 297242
- ↗ www.northlincs.gov.uk/NorthLincs /Education

North Somerset

North Somerset Council, Admissions and Student Funding Team, Town Hall, Walliscote Grove Road, Weston-Super-Mare BS23 1ZZ

- **t A–Gh** 01275 884220
- **Gi–N** 01275 884374
- **O–Z** 01275 888296
- **f** 01275 884168
- **e** awards@n-somerset.gov.uk
- ↗ www.n-somerset.gov.uk

- **North Tyneside**
Student Support Services,
Pametrada Building, Davy Bank, Wallsend,
Tyne and Wear, NE28 6UZ
  t 0191 2 007070
  f 0191 2 007023

- **North Yorkshire**
Student Support Section, North Yorkshire
County Council, County Hall, Northallerton,
North Yorkshire DL7 8AE
AWARDS OFFICE
  t 08453 452153
  f 01609 778611
  e student.support@northyorks.gov.uk
  ⌁ www.northyorks.gov.uk/lifelonglearning

- **Northamptonshire**
Student Support, Northamptonshire County
Council, PO Box 216 John Dryden House,
8–10 The Lakes, Northampton NN4 7DD
STUDENT SUPPORT OFFICE
  t 01604 236290
  t 01604 236292
  f 01604 237414
  e studentsupport@
       northamptonshire.gov.uk

- **Northumberland**
Education Department, Northumberland
County Council, County Hall, Morpeth,
Northumberland NE61 2EF
STUDENT AWARDS OFFICE
  t 01670 533088
  f 01670 533731

- **Nottingham**
Student Awards, Nottingham City LEA,
PO Box 7167, Nottingham NG1 4WD
STUDENT AWARDS OFFICE
  t 01159 154994
  f 01159 154044

- **Nottinghamshire (LEA in pilot)**
Student Support, Nottinghamshire County
Council, County Hall Loughborough Road,
West Bridgford, Nottingham NG2 7QP
STUDENT SUPPORT OFFICE
  t 01159 772277
  f 01159 772437
  e student.support@
       education.nottscc.gov.uk
  ⌁ www.nottscc.gov.uk/education/grants
       /index.htm

- **Oldham**
Student Support, PO Box 40, Civic Centre,
West Street, Oldham OL1 1XJ
  t 01619 113352
  f 01619 114277
  e ecs.studentsupport@oldham.gov.uk

- **Oxfordshire**
Student Support, Learning and Culture,
Oxfordshire County Council, Macclesfield
House, New Road, Oxford OX1 1NA
  t 01865 815433
  f 01865 815109
  e student.support@oxfordshire.gov.uk
  ⌁ www.oxfordshire.gov.uk/index
       /learning/studentsupport.htm

- **Pembrokeshire**
Education Department, Pembrokshire
County Council, St Thomas' Green,
Haverford West, Pembrokeshire SA61 1QZ
STUDENT AWARDS OFFICE
  t 01437 764551

- **Peterborough**
Student Support Service, Cambrideshire
County Council, Shire Hall, Castle Court,
Cambridge CB3 0AP
  t 01223 717942
  f 01223 717771
  e student.finance@cambridgeshire.gov.uk

- **Plymouth**
Student Support Team, Plymouth City Council,
Martins Gate, Bretonside, Plymouth PL4 0AT
  t 01752 253290
  f 01752 255945
  e studenthelp@plymouth.gov.uk
  ⌁ www.plymouth.gov.uk/studentsupport

■ Poole

Student Support, Borough of Poole, Civic Centre, Poole, Dorset BH15 2YE

STUDENT SUPPORT

t 01202 634250
f 01202 633150

■ Portsmouth

Student Support, Portsmouth City Council, Civic Offices, Guildhall Square, Portsmouth PO1 2AR

STUDENT SUPPORT

t 02392 841324
f 02392 841427

■ Powys

Education Department, Powys County Council, Southfields, County Hall, Llandrindod Wells, Powys LD1 5LG

STUDENT AWARDS OFFICE

t 01597 827054, 01597 827360
    01597 827137, 01597 826418
f 01597 827117

■ Reading

Student Support, Reading Borough Council, Civic Offices, Civic Centre, Reading RG1 7TD

STUDENT SUPPORT OFFICERS

t A–H 01189 390556
    T–Z 01189 390552
f 01189 390782

■ Redbridge

Education Office, London Borough of Redbridge, 22–26 Clements Road, Ilford, Essex IG1 1BD

STUDENT SUPPORT

t A–K 02087 084189
    L–Z 02087 084183
f 02087 084193

■ Redcar and Cleveland

Student Support, Redcar and Cleveland Borough Council, PO Box 83 Council Offices, Kirkleatham Street, Redcar TS10 1YA

STUDENT AWARDS OFFICE

t 01642 444118, 01642 444119
f 01642 444122
e student_support@
    redcar-cleveland.gov.uk

■ Rhondda, Cynon, Taff

Awards and Benefits Division, Education and Children's Services, Rhondda Cynon Taff – County Borough Council, Ty Trevithick Abercynon, Mountain Ash, Mid Glamorgan, CF45 4UQ

STUDENT AWARDS OFFICE

t 01443 744151
f 01443 744024

■ Richmond upon Thames

Education Department, London Borough of Richmond upon Thames, Regal House, London Road, Twickenham TW1 3QB

PRINCIPAL GRANTS AND AWARDS OFFICE

t 02088 917588, 02088 917508
f 02088 917714
e student.support@richmond.gov.uk
↗ www.richmond.gov.uk/studentsupport

■ Rochdale

Education Department, PO Box 70, Municipal Offices, Smith Street, Rochdale OL16 1YD

STUDENT SUPPORT

t 01706 865115, 01706 647474
f 01706 658560
e studentsupport@rochdale.gov.uk
↗ www.rochdale.gov.uk/living
    /studentenquiry

■ Rotherham

Student Support Service, Rotherham Metropolitan Borough Council, Norfolk House, Walker Place, Rotherham S65 1AS

STUDENT SUPPORT

t 01709 382121
f 01709 822654
e student.enquiries@rotherham.gov.uk
↗ www.rotherham.gov.uk

■ Rutland

Rutland council, c/o Awards Loans Grants Service, Education Dept, County Hall, Glenfield, Leicester LE3 8SA

STUDENT AWARDS SECTION

t 01162 656376, 01162 656382
f 01162 656400

■ Salford
Student Support Team, Salford Education and Leisure Directorate, Minerva House Pendlebury Road, Swinton, Manchester M27 4EQ

STUDENT SUPPORT
- t 01617 780209 01617 780207
- f 01617 286134
- e student.support@salford.gov.uk
- ↗ www.salford.gov.uk/education

■ Sandwell
Student Finance Direct, Sandwell Metropolitan Borough Council, Shaftesbury House, 402 High Street, West Bromwich B70 9LT

DSA ENQ
- t 01215 698134 (Karen Goddard)
  01215 698183 (Robert Cousins)
  01215 698263 (Stuart Leatherland)
  01215 698110 (Linda Woodall)
  01215 698180 (Ross Priest)
  01215 698149 (Margaret Haywood)
  01215 698271 (Kay Butler)
  01215 698290 (Tracy Rogers, Principal Student Finance Officer)
  01215 698134 (Karen Goddard, Senior Student Finance Officer)
- e studentfinancedirect@sandwell.gov.uk
- ↗ www.sandwell.gov.uk

■ Sefton
Benefits Officer, Student Support Section, Sefton Education Department, Bootle Town Hall, Bootle L20 7AE

STUDENT SUPPORT
- t 01519 343456
- f 01519 343255
- e benefits@education.sefton.gov.uk

■ Sheffield
Student Support Department, Howden House, Floor 3, 1 Union Street, Sheffield S1 2SH
- t A–Mac 01142 735635
  Mad–Z 01142 735796
- f 01142 736279

■ Shropshire
Student Support, Shropshire County Council, Shirehall, Abbey Foregate, Shrewsbury SY2 6ND

STUDENT SUPPORT
- t 01743 254340
- f 01743 254479
- e student_support@shropshire-cc.gov.uk
- ↗ www.shropshireonline.gov.uk /studentsupport.nsf

■ Slough
Student Support Service, Slough Borough Council, Town Hall, Bath Road, Slough SL1 3UQ

STUDENT AWARDS OFFICE
- t 01753 875721
- f 01753 875725
- e studentsupport@slough.gov.uk

■ Solihull
Student Support, Metropolitan Borough of Solihull, PO Box 20, Council House, Solihull B91 3QU

STUDENT SUPPORT
- t 01217 046639
- f 01217 046157
- e studentsupport@solihull.gov.uk

■ Somerset
Student Support, Lifelong Learning Department, County Hall, Taunton, Somerset TA1 4DY
- t

A–Cg	01823 355946 (Carol Gamblin)
Ch–E	01823 355947 (Peter Coward)
F–Hoa	01823 355705 (Matthew Shane)
Hob–Map	01823 355703 (Peter Sadil)
Maq–Po	01823 355702 (James Baker)
Pp–St	01823 355943 (Derek Hector)
Su–Z	01823 355701 (Simon Heritage)
DSA Enq:	01823 355794 (Andrew McGill)

- e studentsupport@somerset.gov.uk
- ↗ www.somerset.gov.uk/education /educservices/studentsupport

■ South Gloucestershire

Student Support Team, South Gloucestershire Council, Bowling Hill, Chipping Sodbury, South Gloucestershire BS37 6JX

SENIOR ADMINISTRATION ASSISTANT

t 01454 863292
f 01454 863263
e educ.grants@southglos.gov.uk

■ South Tyneside

Education Department, South Tyneside Metropolitan Borough Council, Town Hall, South Shields, Tyne and Wear NE33 2RL

STUDENT SUPPORT

t 01914 247719
f 01914 270584

■ Southampton

Student Finance Service, Southampton City Council, Civic Centre, Southampton SO14 7SA

t 02380 833555
f 02380 233756
e student.finance@southampton.gov.uk

■ Southend-on-Sea

Student Support, Southend-on-Sea Borough Council, PO Box 6 Civic Centre, Victoria Avenue, Southend-on-Sea SS2 6ER

STUDENT HELPLINE

t 01245 245900
f 01245 245939

■ Southwark

Student Finance, 15 Spa Road, Bermondsey, London SE16 3QW

t Public and Student Contact:
02075 251514
SLC, institutions and other agencies:
02075 251524 0
f 02075 251546
e kwame.ofusu-sefah@southwark.gov.uk
clinton.hutchinson@southwark.gov.uk
↗ www.southwark.lgfl.net

■ St Helens

St Helens Council, Education and Leisure Services, Student Awards Section, Wesley House, Corporation Street, St Helens, Merseyside WA10 1HF

t 01744 455335, 01744 445414
f 01744 455407
e studentsupport@sthelens.gov.uk

■ Staffordshire

Student Support Service, Education Offices, Tipping Street, Stafford ST16 2DH

t A–C 01785 278936
D–J 01785 278937
K–Sp 01785 278933
Sq–Z 01785 278935
↗ www.staffordshire.gov.uk/studentsupport

■ Stockport

Education Division, Stockport Metropolitan Borough Council, Further Education, Town Hall, Stockport SK1 3XE

STUDENT AWARDS OFFICE

t 01614 743849, 01614 743852
f 01613 556968

■ Stockton-on-Tees

Student Support, Stockton-on-Tees Council, PO Box 228 Municipal Buildings, Church Road, Stockton-on-Tees, TS18 1XE

STUDENT SUPPORT

t 01642 526608
f 01642 393525
e student.support@stockton.gov.uk

■ Stoke-on-Trent

Student Support Applications are dealt with by Staffordshire County Council under an agency agreement. See **Staffordshire**

■ Suffolk

Student Support Office, St Andrew House, County Hall, Ipswich IP4 1LJ

t 01473 584600
f 01473 584636

- **Sunderland**
Finance Service (Awards Unit), Education
Directorate, PO Box 101, Civic Centre,
Sunderland SR2 7DN
STUDENT AWARDS OFFICE
  t 01915 531415, 01915 531480
     01915 531458
  f 01915 531410
  e HESupport@edcom.sunderland.gov.uk

- **Surrey**
Student Support, County Hall, Penrhyn
Road, Kingston-upon-Thames KT1 2EX
HEAD OF STUDENT SUPPORT
  t general enquiries 08456 009009
     A–F 02085 419492
     G–O 02085 419490
     P–W 02085 419494
     X–Z & DSA Enq 02085 419491
  f 02085 419595, 02085 417696
  e student.support.ses@surreycc.gov.uk
  ↗ www.surrey.cc.gov.uk/studentsupport

- **Sutton**
Student Support, London Borough of Sutton,
Learning for Life, The Grove, Carshalton
SM5 3AL
STUDENT SUPPORT
  t 02087 706640
  f 02087 706545
  e sfs@suttonlea.org.uk
  ↗ www.sutton.gov.uk

- **Swansea**
Student Support – Education Department,
City and County of Swansea, County Hall,
Swansea SA1 3SN
STUDENT AWARDS OFFICE
  t 01792 636000
  f 01792 636642
  e student.support@swansea.gov.uk
  ↗ www.swansea.gov.uk

- **Swindon**
Student Support, Swindon Borough Council,
Sandford House, Sandford Street,
Swindon SN1 1QH
STUDENT SUPPORT
  t 01793 463077, 01793 463079
  f 01793 488597

- **Tameside**
Student Awards Section, Tameside
Metropolitan Borough Council, Education
and Cultural Services, Wellington Road,
Ashton-under-Lyne OL6 6DL
STUDENT AWARDS OFFICE
  t 01613 422203, 01613 423215
  f 01613 423260
  e student.awards@mail.tameside.gov.uk
  ↗ www.tameside.gov.uk

- **Telford and Wrekin**
Student Support, Shropshire County Council,
Shirehall, Abbey Foregate, Shrewsbury
SY2 6ND
  t 01743 254340
  f 01743 254479
  e student_support@shropshire-cc.gov.uk
  ↗ www.shropshireonline.gov.uk
     /studentsupport.nsf

- **Thurrock**
Student Support, Thurrock Council, Civic
Offices New Road, Grays, Essex RM17 6SL
STUDENT AWARDS AND BENEFITS OFFICE
  t 01375 652882
  f 01375 652792

- **Torbay**
Student Support, Torbay Borough Council,
Oldway Torquay Road, Paignton,
Devon TQ3 2TE
STUDENT SERVICES
  t A–B 01803 665976 (S Green)
     M–Z 01803 665976 (C Friend)
  f 01803 208225
  e studentservices@torbay.gov.uk

- **Torfaen**
Student Support, Torfen County Borough
Council, County Hall, Cwmbran NP44 2WN
STUDENT AWARDS OFFICE
  t 01633 648122

- **Tower Hamlets**
Education Department, London Borough
of Tower Hamlets, Mulberry Place,
5 Clove Crescent, London E14 2BG
STUDENT SUPPORT
  t 02073 644410, 02073 644239
  f 02073 644311

■ Trafford
Student Support, Trafford MBC,
The Ground Floor, Waterside House,
Waterside, Sale M33 7ZF
STUDENT SUPPORT MANAGER
  t 01619 123166
  f 01619 123317

■ Vale of Glamorgan
Student Support, The Vale of Glamorgan
County Borough Council, Civic Offices,
Holton Road, Barry CF63 4RU
STUDENT SERVICES
  t 01446 709539

■ Wakefield
Pupil and Student Support (Finance),
Wakefield Metropolitan District Council,
County Hall, Wakefield WF1 2QL
  t A–F 01924 305061
     G–O 01924 305075
     P–Z 01924 305625
  f 01924 305611
  e pssf@wakefield.gov.uk

■ Walsall
Student Support, Walsall Metropolitan
Borough Council, The Civic Centre Darwell
Street, Walsall, West Midlands WS1 1DQ
STUDENT AWARDS OFFICE
  t 01922 654040
  f 01922 722322

■ Waltham Forest
Student Support, London Borough of
Waltham Forest, Municipal Office
High Road, Leyton, London E10 5QJ
PRINCIPAL AWARDS OFFICE
  t 02084 965026
  f 02084 985077
  e student.support@edu.lbwf.gov.uk

■ Wandsworth
London Borough of Wandsworth, Student
Finance Section, Town Hall, Wandsworth
High Street, London SW18 2PU
STUDENT SUPPORT
  t 02088 718073
  f 02088 718086
  e studentfinance@wandsworth.gov.uk
  ↗ www.wandsworth.gov.uk/studentfinance

■ Warrington
Student Support Team – Education and
Lifelong Learning Dept, Warrington
Borough Council, New Town House,
Buttermarket Street, Warrington WA1 2NJ
STUDENT AWARDS OFFICE
  t 01925 442993
  f 01925 442969
  e esvstudent@warrington.gov.uk

■ Warwickshire
Student Services, Warwickshire County
Council, Education Department,
22 Northgate Street, Warwick CV34 4SR
STUDENT SERVICES
  t Supplementary Awards 0192 641 8144
     Aaa–Bru 01926 418142
     Brv–Dir 01926 412902
     Dis–Haj 01926 418073
     Elm–Hee 01926 418073
     Hee–Lew 01926 412483
     Lex–Pan 01926 418139
     Pao–Sim 01926 418143
     Sin–Whe 01926 412011
     Whf–Zzz 01926 418144
  f 01926 412627
  e studentawards@warwickshire.gov.uk
  ↗ www.warwickshire.gov.uk
     /studentsupport

■ West Berkshire
Student Support, West Berkshire Council,
Avonbank House, West Street,
Newbury RG14 1BZ
STUDENT SUPPORT
  t A–K 01635 519774
     L–Z 01635 519776
  f 01635 519048

■ West Sussex
Student Support, West Sussex County
Council, County Hall, West Street,
Chichester PO19 1RF
STUDENT SUPPORT
  t 01243 777637
  f 01243 752170

■ Westminster

Student Support, Westminster City Council,
PO Box 240 Westminster City Hall,
64 Victoria Street, London SW1E 6QP

SENIOR AWARDS OFFICE

t 02076 411842
f 02076 413406

■ Wigan

Education Offices, Wigan Borough Council,
Gateway House, Standishgate,
Wigan WN1 1AE

STUDENT SERVICES

t 01942 828903, 01942 828908
f 01942 404151

■ Wiltshire

Student Finance Team, Wiltshire County
Council, County Hall, Bythesea Road,
Trowbridge, Wiltshire BA14 8JB

STUDENT FINANCE MANAGER:
Michael Gamble

t 01225 713891
f 01225 713684
e studentsupport@wiltshire.gov.uk

■ Windsor and Maidenhead

Student Finance, Royal Borough of Windsor
and Maidenhead, Town Hall, St Ives Road,
Maidenhead SL6 1RF

STUDENT SUPPORT

t 01628 796712
f 01628 796685
e student.grants@rbwm.gov.uk
↗ www.rbwm.gov.uk

■ Wirral

Student Support, Metropolitan Borough of
Wirral, Hamilton Building, Conway Street,
Birkenhead CH41 4FD

STUDENT SUPPORT

t 01516 664637
f 01516 664231

■ Wokingham

Student Support, Wokingham District Council,
Education and Cultural Services Dept,
Shute End, Wokingham, Berkshire RG40 1WN

STUDENT SUPPORT

t 01189 746129
f 01189 746259
e student.support@wokingham.gov.uk
↗ www.wokingham.gov.uk/studentsupport

■ Wolverhampton

Pupil and Student Support – Lifelong
Learning Education, Wolverhampton City
Council, Civic Centre, St Peter's Square,
Wolverhampton WV3 1RR

STUDENT SUPPORT

t 01902 554140
f 01902 554218

■ Worcestershire

Student Support Service, Educational
Services Directorate, Worcestershire County
Council, PO Box 73, Worcester WR5 2YA

STUDENT SUPPORT SERVICES

t A–Do 01905 765904
   Dr–Ke 01905 765905
   Kh–Ri 01905 765908
   Ro–Z 01905 765907
f 01905 765660
e studentsupport@worcestershire.gov.uk
↗ www.worcestershire.gov.uk
    /studentsupport

■ Wrexham

Student Support, Wrexham County Borough
Council, TY Henblas, Queens Square,
Wrexham LL13 8AZ

t 01978 297466, 01978 297467
  01978 297480
f 01978 297501
e grahame.hughes@wrexham.gov.uk

■ York

Student Support, City of York Council,
George Hudson Street, York YO1 1ZG

STUDENT SUPPORT OFFICE

t 01904 554251
f 01904 554249
e student.awards@york.gov.uk
↗ www.york.gov.uk/learning/adult
    education/studentsupport.html

Scotland

Students in Scotland apply through the Student Awards Agency for Scotland

■ **The Student Awards Agency for Scotland**
Gyleview House, 3 Redheughs Rigg, Edinburgh EH12 9HH
t 0845 111 1711
e saas.geu@scotland.gsi.gov.uk.
↗ www.student-support-saas.gov.uk

Northern Ireland

Students from Northern Ireland have to make their applications for financial support through their local Education and Library Board:

■ **Belfast Education and Library Board**
40 Academy Street, Belfast BT1 2NQ
↗ www.belb.org.uk

■ **Western Education and Library Board**
Campsie Road, 1 Hospital Road, Omagh BT79 0AW
↗ www.welbni.org

■ **North-Eastern Education and Library Board**
County Hall, 182 Galgorm Road, Ballymena BT42 1HN
↗ www.neelb.org.uk

■ **South-Eastern Education and Library Board**
Grahamsbridge Road, Dundonald, Belfast BT16 0HS
↗ www.seelb.org.uk

■ **Southern Education and Library Board**
3 Charlemont Place, Armagh BT61 9AX
↗ www.selb.org

Useful contacts

The following agencies provide welfare information and support on a range of financial and related issues.

Accommodation

■ Advisory Service for Squatters
Provides useful advice and information on all aspects of squatting.

2 St Paul's Road, London N1 2QN
t 020 7359 8814
 or 0845 644 5814 (local rate)
 (2–6 p.m., Monday to Friday)
f 020 7359 5185
e advice@squat.freeserve.co.uk
↗ www.squat.freeserve.co.uk

■ Chartered Institute of Environmental Health (CIEH)
The CIEH represents local authority environmental health officers and can provide contacts, as well as helpful information about a wide range of public health issues.

Chadwick Court, 15 Hatfields,
London SE1 8DJ
t 020 7928 6006
f 020 7827 5866
e info@cieh.org
↗ www.cieh.org.uk/cieh/

■ CORGI
The Council for Registered Gas Installers is the body that ensures gas engineers are up to standard. They also keep a record of which installers are permitted to carry their logo.

1 Elmwood, Chineham Business Park,
Crockford Lane, Basingstoke, Hants
RG24 8WG
t 0870 401 2300
f 0870 401 2600
e enquiries@corgi-gas.com
↗ www.corgi-gas-safety.com

■ CO Gas Safety
A charity that campaigns on behalf of victims of CO (carbon monoxide) poisoning as well as for improvements to the gas safety regulations. They log CO deaths and can provide guidance if a death occurs.

Lorien House,Common Lane, Claygate,
Surrey KT10 0HY
t 01372 466135
f 01372 468 965
↗ www.charitynet.org/~CO-gas/

■ The Office of the Deputy Prime Minister (ODPM)
The ODPM can be a useful source of information. It also has a free publications service – call 0870 122 6236.

26 Whitehall, London SW1A 2WH
t 020 7944 4400
↗ www.odpm.gov.uk

■ Homeless Link
Campaigns on single person homelessness. Produces a number of publications, including *The Benefits Guide*.

First Floor, 10–13 Rushworth Street,
London SE1 0RB
t 020 7960 3010
↗ www.homeless.org.uk

■ Shelter
Provides publications and training and organises local groups in England.

88 Old Street, London EC1V 9HU
t 020 7505 4699 and
 020 7505 2000 (Main Switchboard)
 SHELTERLINE 0808 800 4444 (24 hour)
e info@shelter.org.uk
↗ www.shelter.org.uk

■ Shelter – Cymru
25 Walter Road, Swansea SA1 5NN
t 01792 469400
↗ www.sheltercymru.org.uk

Shelter – Scotland
4th Floor, Scotiabank House, 6 South
Charlotte Street, Edinburgh EH2 4AW
t 0131 473 7170
↗ www.scotland.shelter.org.uk

Shelter – Northern Ireland
10–12 High Street, Belfast BT1 2BA
t 028 9024 5640
e shelter@cinni.org

Tenancy Deposit Scheme
Housing Ombudsman Service, Norman House,
105–109 Strand, London WC2R 0AA
t 0845 601 1200
f 020 7836 3900
e tds@ihos.org.uk
↗ www.ihos.org.uk/tds/

4 Children
Formerly the Kid's Club Network.
t 020 7512 2112
↗ www.4children.org.uk

Childline
24-hour free helpline for children.
t 0800 1111

Daycare Trust
21 St George's Road, London SE1 6ES
CHILDCARE HOTLINE 020 7840 3350
    (10 a.m.–5 p.m., Monday to Friday)
t 020 7840 3350
e info@daycaretrust.org.uk
↗ www.daycaretrust.org.uk

Gingerbread – England and Wales
ADVICE LINE 0800 018 4318
    (9 a.m.–5 p.m., Monday to Friday)
t 020 7488 9300
↗ www.gingerbread.org.uk

Gingerbread – Scotland
1014 Argyle Street, Glasgow G3 8LX
t 0141 576 5085
↗ www.gingerbread.org.uk

Gingerbread – Northern Ireland
169 University Street, Belfast BT7 1HR
ADVICE LINE 0808 808 8090
t 028 9023 1417
↗ www.gingerbreadni.org

National Childminding Association
8 Masons Hill, Bromley, Kent BR2 9EY
t 020 8464 6164
e info@ncma.org.uk
↗ www.ncma.org.uk

One Parent Families
255 Kentish Town Road, London NW5 2LX
t 020 7428 5400
e info@oneparentfamilies.org.uk
↗ www.oneparentfamilies.org.uk

Debt

- **Child Poverty Action Group (CPAG)**
94 White Lion Street, London N1 9PF
  - **t** 020 7837 7979
    HELPLINE 020 7833 4627
    (for advisers only)
  - ↗ www.cpag.org.uk

- **Consumer Credit Counselling Service**
  - **t** FREEPHONE 0800 1381111
    (8 a.m.–8 p.m., Monday to Friday)
  - ↗ www.cccs.co.uk

- **Credit Action Student Freephone Helpline**
  - **t** 0800 591 084

- **National Consumer Council**
20 Grosvenor Gardens, London SW1W 0DH
  - **t** 020 7730 3469
  - ↗ www.ncc.org.uk

- **National Debtline**
  - **t** 0808 808 4000
    (9 a.m.–9 p.m., Monday to Friday;
    9.30 a.m.–1 p.m. Saturday)
  - ↗ www.nationaldebtline.co.uk

Law

- **Commission for Racial Equality**
St Dunstan's House, 201–211 Borough High Street, London SE1 1GZ
  - **t** 020 7939 0000
  - **e** info@cre.gov.uk
  - ↗ www.cre.gov.uk

- **Disability Law Service**
Ground Floor, 39–45 Cavell House, Cavell Street, London E1 2BP
  - **t** 020 7791 9800
    Text/Minicom 020 7791 9801

- **Equal Opportunities Commission**
Arndale House, Arndale Centre,
Manchester M4 3EQ
  - **t** 0845 601 5901
  - **e** info@eoc.org.uk
  - ↗ www.eoc.org.uk

- **Free Representation Unit**
Helps provide free legal representation to those who cannot afford to pay and where Legal Aid is not available. London only.
4th Floor, Peer House, 8–14 Verulam Street, London WC1X 8LZ
  - **t** 020 7831 0692
  - **e** admin@fru.org.uk
  - ↗ www.fru.org.uk

- **Liberty (National Council for Civil Liberties)**
21 Tabard Street, London SE1 4LA
  - **t** 020 7403 3888
  - ↗ www.liberty-human-rights.org.uk

Overseas students

■ **Joint Council for the Welfare of Immigrants**
115 Old Street, London EC1V 9RT
t 02 (0) 7251 8708
ADVICELINE 020 7251 8706
(2–5 p.m., Tuesday and Thursday)
e info@jcwi.org.uk
↗ www.jcwi.org.uk

■ **Refugee Council**
Head Office, 240–250 Ferndale Road,
London SW9 8BB
t 020 7346 6700
ADVICE LINE 020 7346 6777
(10 a.m.–1 p.m., 2 p.m.–5 p.m.,
Monday to Friday, except Wednesday)
INFORMATION LINE 020 7820 3085
(10 a.m.–1 p.m., Monday to Friday,
except Thursday)
e info@refugeecouncil.org.uk
↗ www.refugeecouncil.org.uk

■ **United Kingdom Council on Overseas Student Affairs (UKCOSA)**
Offers advice and information on immigration and other issues affecting overseas students.
9–17 St Albans Place, London N1 0NX
t 020 7288 4330
↗ www.ukcosa.org.uk

European students

For details of financial support for study in England and Wales, contact:

■ **DfES European Team**
2F-Area B, Mowden Hall, Staindrop Road,
Darlington DL3 9BG
t 01325 391199
e euteam@dfes.gsi.gov.uk
↗ www.dfes.gov.uk/studentsupport
/eustudents
(The DfES's website contains information specific for each EU country.)

For details of financial support for study in Scotland, contact:

■ **The Student Awards Agency for Scotland**
Gyleview House, 3 Redheughs Rigg,
Edinburgh EH12 9HH
t 0845 111 1711
e saas.geu@scotland.gsi.gov.uk
↗ www.saas.gov.uk

For details of financial support for study in Northern Ireland, contact:

■ **The Awards Section Belfast Education and Library Board**
40 Academy Street, Belfast BT1 2NQ
t 028 9056 4237
↗ www.student-support.org.uk

■ **European Commission Representation in the United Kingdom**
8 Storey's Gate, London SW1P 3AT
t 020 7973 1992
f 020 7973 1900 / 1910
↗ www.cec.org.uk

Scotland and Scottish students

■ **NUS Scotland**
29 Forth Street, Edinburgh EH1 3LE
t 0131 556 6598
e nus-scot@dircon.co.uk
↗ www.nusonline.co.uk/scotland

■ **Scottish Further Education Funding Council**
Scottish Funding Councils for Further and Higher Education, Donaldson House, 97 Haymarket Terrace, Edinburgh EH12 5HD
t 0131 313 6500
↗ www.sfefc.ac.uk

■ **The Student Awards Agency for Scotland**
Gyleview House, 3 Redheughs Rigg, Edinburgh EH12 9HH
t 0845 111 1711 (8.30 a.m. – 5 p.m.)
f 0131 244 5887
e saas.geu@scotland.gsi.gov.uk
↗ www.saas.gov.uk

■ **The Student Loans Company (Scotland) Ltd**
100 Bothwell Street, Glasgow G2 7JD
t 0800 405010 (calls are free)
↗ www.slc.co.uk

Northern Ireland and Northern Irish students

NUS–USI, 29 Bedford Street, Belfast BT2 7EJ
t 028 9024 4641
f 028 9043 9659
e info@nistudents.org
↗ www.nistudents.org

■ **Educational Guidance Service for Adults (EGSA)**
4th Floor, 40 Linenhall Street, Belfast BT2 8BA
t 028 9024 4274
f 028 9027 1507
e info@egsa.org.uk
↗ www.egsa.org.uk

■ **Department for Employment and Learning**
Student Support Branch, Room 407, 4th Floor, Adelaide House, 39–49 Adelaide Street, Belfast BT2 8FD
t 028 90 257710
f 028 90 257747
e studentsupport@delni.gov.uk
↗ www.delni.gov.uk

■ **Student Awards**

Belfast
Belfast Education and Library Board, 40 Academy Street, Belfast BT1 2NQ
t 028 9056 4237
f 028 9033 1714
e student.awards@belb.co.uk
↗ www.belb.org.uk

Ards, Castlereagh, Down, Lisburn, North Down
South Eastern Education and Library Board, Grahamsbridge Road, Dundonald, Belfast BT16 2HS
t 028 9056 6200
f 028 9056 6267
e student.awards@seelb.org.uk
↗ www.seelb.org.uk

**Antrim, Ballymena, Ballymoney,
Carrickfergus, Coleraine, Larne,
Magherafelt, Moyle, Newtownabbey**
North Eastern Education and Library Board,
County Hall, 182 Galgorm Road, Ballymena,
Co. Antrim BT42 1HN
t   028 2565 5025
f   028 2564 3674
e   student.awards@neelb.org.uk
↗ www.neelb.org.uk

**Fermanagh, Limavady, Londonderry,
Omagh, Strabane**
Western Education and Library Board,
Campsie House, 1 Hospital Road,
Omagh, Co. Tyrone BT79 0AW
t   028 8241 1499
f   028 8241 1233
e   student.awards@welbni.org
↗ www.welbni.org

**Armagh, Banbridge, Cookstown,
Craigavon, Dungannon, Newry and Mourne**
Southern Education and Library Board,
3 Charlemont Place, The Mall,
Armagh BT61 9AX
t   028 3751 2432
f   028 3751 2490
e   student.awards@selb.org
↗ www.selb.org

■ **Skill NI – National Bureau for
   Students with Disabilities**
Unit 2, Jennymount Court,
North Derby Street, Belfast BT15 3HN
t (& MINICOM) 028 9028 7000
f   028 9028 7002
e   admin@skillni.org.uk

■ **The Association of Commonwealth
   Universities**
36 Gordon Square, London WC1H 0PF
t   020 7380 6700
f   020 7387 2655
e   info@acu.ac.uk
↗ www.acu.ac.uk
(See page 102 for details on their scholarships.)

■ **The Africa Educational Trust**
Africa Centre, 38 King Street, London
WC2E 8JR
e   aet@cwcom.net
↗ www.africaeducationaltrust.mcmail.com

The AET makes small awards to African
students who are in short-term financial
difficulties, close to the completion of their
course. They also give full- and part-time
scholarships in continental Europe. Written
applications only. Free educational advice
for African students, refugees and asylum
seekers, arranged by appointment.

■ **Education Action International**
14 Dufferin Street, London EC1Y 8PD.
t   020 7426 5800 (general enquiries).
↗ www.education-action.org

EAI makes small awards to refugees and
asylum seekers.

■ **The Hammond Trust**
International Student Service Limited,
The British Council, 58 Whitworth Street,
Manchester M1 6BB
t   0161 957 7755

Administered by the British Council, the
Hammond Trust is able to award small
grants to students from Asia. However,
grants are awarded only during the last six
months of study to help students complete a
course or research project.

- **Refugee Education and Training Advisory Service (RETAS)**
14 Dufferin Street, London EC1Y 8PD
HELPLINE 020 7426 5801
  (2.30 p.m.–5 p.m.,
  Tuesdays and Thursdays only)
↗ www.education-action.org

For advice and information on sources of funding for refugees and asylum seekers.

- **The SinoBritish Fellowship Trust**
c/o The British Academy, 10 Carlton House Terrace, London SW1Y 5AH
t 020 7969 5200
↗ www.britac.ac.uk/funding/guide/intl/sbft.html

Gives small awards to postgraduate students from the Far East. Candidates should be over 27 years of age.

- **Studying in the UK: Sources of funding for International Students**
Available online or from
The British Council, 10 Spring Gardens London SW1A 2BN
t 0161 957 7755
e general.enquiries@britishcouncil.org
↗ www.britishcouncil.org

- **UKCOSA: The Council for International Education**
7–9 St Alban's Place, London N1 0NX
HELPLINE 020 7107 9922
  (1–4 p.m., Monday to Friday)
↗ www.ukcosa.org.uk

Offers advice on financial difficulties and may be able to suggest additional sources of help.

Postgraduates

- **Arts and Humanities Research Board**
Whitefriars, Lewins Mead, Bristol BS1 2AE
t 0117 987 6543
f 0117 987 6544
↗ www.ahrb.ac.uk

- **The Natural Environment Research Council**
Polaris House, North Star Avenue, Swindon SN2 1EU
t 01793 411500
f 01793 411501
↗ www.nerc.ac.uk

- **Medical Research Council**
20 Park Crescent, London W1B 1AL
t 020 7636 5422
f 020 7436 6179
↗ www.mrc.ac.uk

- **Particle Physics and Astronomy Research Council**
Polaris House, North Star Avenue, Swindon SN2 1SZ
t 01793 442000
f 01793 442125
↗ www.pparc.ac.uk

- **Engineering and Physical Sciences Research Council**
Polaris House, North Star Avenue, Swindon SN2 1ET
t 01793 444000
  HELPLINE 01793 444100
e studentships@epsrc.ac.uk
↗ www.epsrc.ac.uk

- **Biotechnology and Biological Sciences Research Council**
Polaris House, North Star Avenue, Swindon SN2 1UH
t 01793 413200
f 01793 413201
↗ www.bbsrc.ac.uk

- **Economic and Social Research Council**
Polaris House, North Star Avenue,
Swindon SN2 1UJ
  - t 01793 413000
  - f 01793 413001
  - ↗ www.esrc.ac.uk

Funding for courses in England

- **NHS Student Grants Unit**
22 Plymouth Road, Blackpool FY3 7JS
  - t 01253 655 655
  - f 01253 655 660
  - e nhs-sgu@ukonline.co.uk

- **Student Loans Company Ltd**
100 Bothwell Street, Glasgow G2 7JD
  - t 0800 40 50 10 (freephone)
    MINICOM 0800 085 3950
  - f 0141 306 2005
  - ↗ www.slc.co.uk

Funding for courses in Wales

- **The NHS (Wales) Student Awards Unit**
2nd Floor, Golate House, 101 St Mary Street, Cardiff CF10 1DX
  - t 02920 261 495

Funding for courses in Scotland

- **Student Awards Agency for Scotland**
Gyleview House, 3 Redheughs Rigg, Edinburgh EH12 9HH
  - t 0845 111 1711 (8.30 a.m.–5 p.m.)
  - f 0131 244 5887
  - e saas.geu@scotland.gsi.gov.uk
  - ↗ www.saas.gov.uk

Funding for courses in Northern Ireland

- **Department for Health, Social Service and Public Safety**
Bursary Administration Unit, Central Services Agency, 25 Adelaide Street, Belfast BT2 8FH
  - t 028 9055 3661
  - f 028 9055 3689

General information

■ **Free booklet available on request from:**
The Department of Health Publications
PO Box 777, London SE1 6XH
t 08701 555 455
f 01623 724524
e doh@prolog.uk.com

■ **NHS Careers Helpline**
t 0845 6060 655

Applications for study should be made to:

■ **UCAS** (for degree level study)
t 0870 1122211
↗ www.ucas.com

or

■ **NMAS** (for diploma level study)
Rose Hill, New Barn Lane, Cheltenham
Glos GL52 3LZ
t 0870 1122206
↗ www.nmas.ac.uk

■ **Department for Education and Skills (DfES)**
t 0870 000 2288
TEXTPHONE 01928 794 274
MINICOM 0845 6055560
PUBLICATIONS 0800 731 9133
e info@dfes.gsi.gov.uk
www.dfes.gov.uk
The booklet *Financial Support for Higher Education Students in 2004/5* is available in print and on the website.

■ **Teacher Training Agency**
t 020 7925 3700,
0845 6000 991
MINICOM 01245 454 343
e teaching@ttainfo.co.uk
www.useyourheadteach.gov.uk
For general information and details of the Graduate and Registered Teacher Programmes.

■ **Teaching Information Line**
t 0845 6000 991 for further details on teaching in England and Wales. There is also a Welsh language line on 0845 6000 992.

■ **Fast Track Programme Information**
↗ www.fasttrackteaching.gov.uk

Health costs

- **Department of Health Stores**
  PO Box 777, London SE1 6XH
  t 08701 555 455
  f 01623 724524
  e doh@prolog.uk.com

- **Prescription Pricing Authority
  (PPA) – Patient Services**
  t 0845 850 11 66
  ↗ www.ppa.org.uk
  The PPA will advise students on low-income
  scheme claims.

Disclaimer

While we have taken every care to ensure that all information was accurate at the time of writing, readers are advised to check that the information we give is relevant to their own personal circumstances. The situation with student finance remains fluid, so readers are advised to check the latest legislative provision before making any decisions. The best way to do this is through their local NUS officer.

We have also do our best to ensure that the e-mail addresses and URLs for external websites referred to in this book are correct and active at the time of going to press. However, we have no responsibility for them and can make no guarantee that an e-mail address or website will remain live, nor do we bear responsibility for the content of those sites.

Acknowledgements

Especial thanks to David Malcolm of the NUS for his invaluable help in the technical editing of this book.

Thanks also to Dan Ashley, Lisa Darnell, Lindsey Fidler Baker, Kat Fletcher, Penny Gardiner, Fran Owen, Bryony Newhouse, Ian Pindar and Ben Siegle.

And, as always, to Nikki and Sammy Sturzaker.

Index